ADVANCE PRAISE

"Jesse Cole is a one-in-a-million guy. He is a wildly successful entrepreneur. He slaps innovation in the face with more
innovation. Jesse's extraordinary energy and knowledge is
coupled with true humility, humor, and entertainment. Find
Your Yellow Tux is highly entertaining and a must-read for
every entrepreneur. Read it today. You will only regret it if
you don't!"

—MIKE MICHALOWICZ, AUTHOR OF *PROFIT FIRST*

"Jesse is a fearless, bold, and wildly innovative entrepreneur,
and his story teaches valuable lessons for anyone wanting to
succeed in business and in life. Find Your Yellow Tux is truly
a textbook on success. I highly recommend it!"

—JOE CALLOWAY, AUTHOR OF *BE THE*
BEST AT WHAT MATTERS MOST

"You should not only read this book, but you should also live by this great life source by Jesse Cole. This book is a roadmap to happiness and success, and it will change your routines from 'not productive' to 'amazing.' If you want to achieve things you might never have thought possible, it's time you put on your yellow tux!"

—TIM CONNOR, GLOBAL SPEAKER
AND BEST-SELLING AUTHOR

"From the minute I picked up Find Your Yellow Tux, I knew it was something special. Jesse is a born storyteller, and his story will inspire anyone to stop standing still and start standing out."

—PAT WILLIAMS, ORLANDO MAGIC SENIOR
VICE PRESIDENT AND AUTHOR OF *COACH
WOODEN'S FORGOTTEN TEAM*

"I've worked with leaders and business owners all over the world, and Jesse is a leader who stands out. Find Your Yellow Tux is a must-read. Not only does it share Jesse's amazing story, but it also paves the way for leaders to create their own path. Read it and start standing out today!"

—JON GORDON, BEST-SELLING AUTHOR OF
THE ENERGY BUS AND *THE CARPENTER*

"A word of warning: Find Your Yellow Tux wasn't written for somebody who wants to stand still. Instead, if you want to jolt yourself and your business, grab hold of Find Your Yellow Tux with both hands, read it as fast as you can—devour it—and, by all means, revel in the journey.

—JON SPOELSTRA, BEST-SELLING AUTHOR
OF *MARKETING OUTRAGEOUSLY*

"Take a market people have given up on. Add equal parts passion, perspiration, and creativity; shaken (not stirred) with personality. Read this book. Stand back. Have fun."

—MIKE VEECK, CO-OWNER OF THE ST. PAUL SAINTS

FIND YOUR YELLOW TUX

FIND YOUR YELLOW TUX

HOW TO BE SUCCESSFUL BY STANDING OUT

JESSE COLE

LIONCREST
PUBLISHING

FIND YOUR YELLOW TUX
How to Be Successful by Standing Out

ISBN   978-1-61961-846-6 *Paperback*
      978-1-61961-845-9 *Ebook*

Dedicated to my past and my future:

My dad and my baby on the way.

CONTENTS

FOREWORD

BY DAN MILLER

I arrived an hour and a half early for the ball game. Not being a sports fan, this was the first real ball game of my life. I'm a businessman, and I was not here because of my love of the game. I was here because I had heard an interview with Jesse Cole, owner of the Savannah Bananas, and I was more than a little intrigued. I contacted him to learn more; he invited me to a game that very night.

Fans were already in line. But there seemed to be no consistency in this audience. I saw kids in strollers and old guys in walkers and wheelchairs. I saw those who were obviously wealthy and those who may have been homeless. I talked to people of varied ethnicities and races. Some were dressed in the finest clothes money can buy and some were there in shorts and flip-flops.

What kind of business was this? There was no clear target audience, no concise demographic, and it was not even clear these people understood baseball. How was this possible—that over four thousand people showed up on short notice, purchased tickets, spent lots more money inside, and seemed to be having the time of their lives?

And then I met the man in the yellow tux. He walked me around the park—greeting fans and employees at every step. And the phenomenon that made no logical sense at first glance began to make sense after all.

Here was a guy who understands being different—who understands the power of standing out in a sea of uniformity, and who is not afraid to try the outrageous or something that's never been done before. And in the process, raving fans are created. People who are more than paying customers. Rather, these are people who will fight for tickets, who will show up early, who will purchase and proudly wear the branded clothing, wave the banners and buy the hot dogs and beer just to be part of the in-crowd.

As a student of marketing, I started to recognize the unique business model I was seeing. I am an author and career/life coach. Put in a quick Google search for career coach and it instantly produces 318 million results. Where am I in that list? I have no idea. It's impossible to stand out in that broad category. But my business name is 48 Days, based on my best-selling book, *48 Days to the Work You Love*. Put "48 Days" in a search, and seventeen of the first twenty listings point right to my business. No fancy SEO, just a distinctive message. Lots of career coaches tell you how to change your life and work, but I'm the guy who says you can do it in forty-eight days, if you create a plan and act on it.

You are now reading one of the wildest, most innovative, inside looks into what it takes to be distinctive and available today.

Find Your Yellow Tux will give you a behind-the-scenes perspective on what it takes to stand out in a noisy world, move into a stale and diminishing business arena, and incite energy and enthusiasm that will be the envy of any rivals. This book is not about baseball—it's about creating a business with customers who are more than purchasers of a product or service. This book will show you how to make those customers loyal fans who promote your brand and create new customers in ways that are envied by those frustrated with the latest marketing secrets and social media techniques.

You'll be encouraged that when failure is looming, you can choose to see opportunity.

You'll be reminded that "normal" is not a desirable position. Being your unique self can open doors of opportunity, joy, and fulfillment that others miss.

You'll see ways to stand out in any industry or profession.

I took four pages of notes that night at the ball game. I didn't keep track of runs, errors, or players' names. But I saw a six-month-old baby honored as baby of the night, ladies given roses during break times, inflatable monkeys being bounced around the crowd, a five-year-old kid hit a "home run," and a blindfolded guy searching for a $20 bill on his hands and knees in front of four thousand screaming fans. And I saw a successful business owner waiting outside for the fans *as they were leaving*, seizing yet one more opportunity to connect personally and thank them for coming.

That's what finding your yellow tux is all about. I trust you'll find yours in the pages you are about to read.

—DAN MILLER, NEW YORK TIMES BEST-SELLING
AUTHOR, *48 DAYS TO THE WORK YOU LOVE*

EULOGY

Success without fulfillment is the ultimate failure.

TONY ROBBINS

If you were to die today, would you be happy with the life you lived and the legacy you left?

This question changed my life. It inspired me to evaluate my life based on fulfillment.

So to begin this book, I'd like to share my eulogy.

Jesse Cole was the ultimate showman who entertained millions by bringing energy, enthusiasm, and enjoyment to everything he touched. A person who inspired millions to challenge the status quo, to be different, and to live the life of their dreams. A person who truly cared for others, was always there for anyone, who would give them every-

thing he had. And the most loving husband and father to his wife and kids. He devoted his life to them and made them happy.

If you were to write yours right now, what would it say?

This is where I ask you to start.

SUIT UP

You don't have to see the whole staircase. Just take the first step.

MARTIN LUTHER KING JR.

I was scared out of my mind.

It was February 2016. My wife, Emily, and I were sleeping on an air mattress in a one-bedroom duplex on Tybee Island, just outside of Savannah, Georgia.

The ceilings leaked. Our roommates were cockroaches. Our grocery budget was enough for some ramen and crackers. Okay, maybe just ramen. It wasn't exactly what you would call our dream house.

Actually, just a few months prior, we kissed our dream house goodbye—along with our savings accounts and our credit score—all in a make-or-break effort to take our young business to the next level.

Whenever you take a risk like that, the sleepless nights are sure to follow. Most nights found us staring blankly at the ceiling or walking laps around the house. We wondered how we got to this point. We wondered how we could afford to keep going. More than anything, we wondered whether our massive risk would pay off.

The next day, we would find out. The next day, the world would meet the Savannah Bananas, the first baseball team named after a fruit.

THERE'S NO SUCH THING AS AN OVERNIGHT SUCCESS

Over the previous decade, we had been trying a lot of new things with our first college ball team, the Gastonia Grizzlies, in North Carolina. In the process, we learned two things: that different wins, and nothing beats attention. Those two lessons were front and center in our minds as we prepared to launch our new team. After ten years, it had all come down to this.

We had high hopes for our crazy little college-level, summer team. Even with our name, we had decided to do something dramatically different. While everyone else was naming their team after animals or other fierce things, we went with a banana.

The whole concept was so bizarre, so out there, and so *fun*, that we knew we had created something special.

On the other hand, we also knew our newly adopted community in Savannah might not be ready for it or feel the same way—at least, not right away.

PREPARING FOR THE WORST

If you're like me, you always have a vision of how things are going to go in situations like that. Actually, if you're really like me, you have several competing visions of how things could go right or wrong.

I figured the gathered press and community would respond in one of three ways: they would cheer us, boo us, or fall silent. I'd be fine with either the cheering or the booing. At least that way I'd have a response.

However, if they stayed silent—if they didn't react at all—that meant they didn't get it. And if they didn't get it, our bananas were as good as boiled.

Not that we were going to let that stop us.

By this point in our career, we were used to some adversity. Over the course of several years, we had turned around a failing franchise in Gastonia into one of the highest-attended, college summer teams in the country. In the process, we started to change the way people thought about baseball in the South.

So, while we hoped for the best, we prepared for the worst. We spent two days brainstorming and drilling down with our staff on how to respond. We imagined a flood of nasty emails and phone calls from people unhappy with our name.

We had responses planned for everything we could think of. But as we would learn in the days that followed, nothing that we planned for ever actually happened.

MANAGING THE MISFIRES

You can do all the planning you want, but it's not until you actually do something that you have to react.

We thought we had done a good job keeping things under wraps. I even avoided wearing my signature yellow tux to avoid dropping any hints. But a few hours before the big launch, one of the top directors in the city came up to me and said, "So, you're going with the 'Bananas,' huh?"

I looked at him like a deer in headlights. All I could get out was, "What?"

"Our staff saw that you registered a trademark for the Savannah Bananas. Good luck with *that*," he said.

Well, I thought, that was a surprise.

Not too long after that, someone posted a screenshot of our Bananas hats on Facebook. Apparently, this hacker wanted to spoil our big announcement. Every time we deleted the post, they just kept reposting it.

Finally, we sent the hacker a message. "Can you please wait two hours?" we said. "We'll send you a free hat if you do."

Thankfully, it worked, but not without teaching us a lesson first. You may have a vision of how things are going to go, but they're bound to take you in a different direction. And when they do, it's up to you to react.

THE GRAND UNVEILING

Finally, the big moment came. As our team president, Jared, announced the Bananas to the world, I stood there on stage with my camera, filming the crowd's responses. First, the faces in the crowd started breaking into smiles. Then, after we unveiled our logo, the room cheered—well, most of them anyway.

A few minutes later, Emily ran up to me in excitement.

"Jesse, you'll never believe what's happening," she said. "We're almost out of shirts!"

"What do you mean?" I said.

Emily explained that we were selling a shirt every couple of seconds online and to customers all over the world. Never mind that the original order of shirts misspelled "Banannas," and we had to max out our credit cards for emergency replacements the week before. Oh, and we had no idea how to navigate bulk and international shipping systems. We lost a lot of money fulfilling that first round of orders.

In other good news, our announcement made us the top trending topic on Twitter. First, *SportsCenter* ran a special on us, and then *Yahoo! Sporting News* and *BuzzFeed* followed suit.

While the national press was soaking it up, the Savannah community was decidedly less excited. And boy, did they want us to know about it. Hundreds of people sent us messages online to let us know they were planning on staying home and boycotting the team. It's cool to be the trending topic on Twitter, but it's not as cool when you realize that half of that attention is coming from trolls.

"Whoever came up with that name should be fired and ridden out of town on a rail!"

"This is an embarrassment to the city of Savannah."

"The owner doesn't know anything about baseball. Pathetic name and organization."

"The single, most ridiculous, insulting, hideous, embarrassing, outlandish name for a baseball team. You'll be giving away tickets to keep the morale of the team up!"[1]

And that was that: the Bananas' first day in Savannah.

We didn't exactly stick the landing, but the hard part was done. And in my experience, *done* is better than *perfect*. I was now free to start losing sleep over something else.

WHO CARES ABOUT YOUR BUSINESS?

Whether you're running a summer league baseball team, a law firm, or a tech startup, chances are you're going to be losing sleep over something. Running your own business isn't easy. In fact, 50 percent of businesses fail

---

1 You like mean tweets? One of my other favorites said that we "lacked a peel." At least that had a good pun. You can watch me and the rest of the Bananas staff read more mean tweets on YouTube (keywords: "Savannah Bananas Mean Tweets").

in the first year, and 96 percent of businesses fail in the first ten years.[2]

BUT WHY?

We can't blame the economy. The Dow Jones has rebounded nicely since its collapse in 2008, and so has the unemployment rate. There's money to be made and plenty of people to help you make it. Yet, for far too many businesses, the story is over before it even begins.

The truth of the matter is that we business owners aren't giving anyone a reason to care. There are plenty of stats to back this up, but here's my favorite: 70 percent of employees aren't engaged at work. Seventy percent![3]

That's 70 percent of people who feel stuck. Seventy percent of people who sit in traffic every day unhappy and unfulfilled. Seventy percent who are standing still, looking for something better but unsure of how to go about getting it.

---

2   Simon Crompton. "Reddit, Kodak Reveal Why 96% of Businesses Fail Within 10 Years." *YFS Magazine*. (August 20, 2015). http://yfsmagazine.com/2015/08/20/reddit-kodak-reveal-why-96-of-businesses-fail-within-10-years/

3   Amy Adkins. "Majority of US Employees Not Engaged Despite Gains in 2014." *Gallup News*. (January 28, 2015). http://news.gallup.com/poll/181289/majority-employees-not-engaged-despite-gains-2014.aspx

IF YOU DON'T CARE, WHO DOES?

Here's something I've learned in my ten-plus years in the entertainment industry: Forget the business you're in. Forget your industry. Forget your market. Forget your location. If you can find your yellow tux, you can find success.

What is your yellow tux? It's the one thing that makes you and your business stand out—the best version of your*self*.

Just look at the Bananas. No one thought it was a good idea to bring another baseball team to Savannah. Why would they? No ball club had *ever* enjoyed sustained success in that town.

For ninety years at Grayson Stadium, games played by teams like the Sand Gnats, the Cardinals, and the Braves ranked among the least attended in their league. These weren't college-level teams like us. These were bona fide Minor League Baseball teams. They had the prestige, pedigree, and resources you'd expect from a billion-dollar brand—and not one of them could figure out how to make it work.

Sure, you could chalk some of this up to baseball's declining popularity in America. For years, baseball brought in plenty of revenue, but it hasn't exactly been winning over new generations of fans. It's a dying sport. Participation in

Little League programs continues to drop, and the average baseball fan is creeping up on their retirement years.[4]

When we brought our particular brand of baseball to Savannah, we knew the odds were stacked against us. I mean, come on—most people don't even know what a summer college league *is*.

However, where other people see failure, I see opportunity. I'm never thinking about what things *should* be. I'm thinking about what they *could* be. We knew that if we gave people a reason to care, we could succeed on our own terms.

So far, it's worked. In our first season, we sold out seven of our first eight games—and then seventeen of our first twenty-two—on our way to a Coastal Plain League championship. In 2017, we sold out every game, which was a feat no summer college team had ever achieved. This kind of popularity has led to even more national recognition.[5] And now, as of this writing, our waitlist for ticket packages for the 2018 season numbers in the thousands!

---

4   Marc Fisher. "Baseball Is Struggling to Hook Kids—and Risks Losing Fans to Other Sports." *The Washington Post.* (April 5, 2015). https://www.washingtonpost.com/sports/nationals/baseballs-trouble-with-the-youth-curve--and-what-that-means-for-the-game/2015/04/05/2da36dca-d7e8-11e4-8103-fa84725dbf9d_story.html

5   For instance, MSNBC ran a great feature story on us in 2017 (Google keywords: "MSNBC Fans Are Going Bananas for Baseball").

Until the Bananas came around, this kind of success was unheard of in our industry. But in a "bad market," in a bad industry, we've succeeded where others have failed.

EMBRACING THE CARNIVAL

At Fans First Entertainment, there's no big secret to the success we've enjoyed. Put simply, we make things fun.

That's the trick to finding success as an entrepreneur or business owner. But make no mistake, having fun takes work—and a plan.

GET A LITTLE CRAZY

Watching the Bananas is like attending a carnival that happens to break out into a baseball game. That's no accident. Our motto is, "Fans first. Entertain always." We reject the idea that baseball is inherently boring, and we do everything in our power to fill every moment with something fun and different.

Remember that scene in *The Sandlot* where the official Little League team rolls up on the sandlot boys and starts talking trash to each other? Well, we *had* to film our version of that when the Grizzlies and the Bananas faced off in 2017. There's nothing like watching two grown men call each other names like "scab eater," "butt sniffer," and "pus licker"—all with the kind of bravado you'd expect from a twelve-year-old boy.[6]

If *Sandlot* parodies aren't your style, we've got plenty else going on in our circus. Perhaps you enjoy watching grown-ass men dress up as French maids, come out to "Lady Marmalade,"[7] and scandalously dust off those dirty, dirty bases. Maybe you like watching the Grim Reaper— the official sponsor of the visiting dugout—come out to the Undertaker's theme and taunt the opposing players. Maybe you like strange giveaways like our "Dig to China" night, where the winning participant earned a one-way ticket to China—and nothing else. No hotel, no return flight home, no spending money, nothing.[8]

I have three posters in my office: one of baseball legend Bill Veeck, one of circus mastermind P.T. Barnum, and one of Mr. Small World himself, Walt Disney. These are my heroes, and as you will see throughout the book, their ideas and stories have driven me to become who I am today.

---

6   You're killing me, Smalls, if you don't watch this YouTube video (keywords: "Savannah Bananas Sandlot Parody").

7   Here, why not jam out to this *Moulin Rouge* classic by Christina Aguilera, Li'l Kim, Mya, and Pink (YouTube keywords: "Moulin Rouge Lady Marmalade").

8   This giveaway was met with no small amount of confusion. At the end of the day, she opted for a cruise for two instead.

WAIT, WHO AM I AGAIN?

Allow me to introduce myself. I'm Jesse Cole, the Yellow Tux Guy. I own Fans First Entertainment, the parent company for our two Coastal Plain League teams, the Gastonia Grizzlies and the Savannah Bananas.

We're proud of what our teams have accomplished so far. Both have set multiple attendance records in their league, and both have led their cities to championship seasons in the Coastal Plain League. In the process, my wife and I went from eating ramen on a blow-up mattress to running a multimillion-dollar entertainment company.

If you had told me ten years ago that I'd own six yellow tuxedos and be the ringleader of a big baseball circus, I would have looked at you like you were crazy—then I would have asked you what your secret was.

You're going to learn plenty about my story in the chapters to come, but for now, here's the quick version. I grew up playing baseball in a baseball family in Massachusetts. I moved to the South on a baseball scholarship, where things were going great, until my arm decided I wasn't going to pitch anymore. I actually have a video of the exact moment when I learned my career was over. As grateful as I am for the life that I have, that video still isn't easy for me to watch.

Anyway, from there, an internship with a ball club in Spartanburg, South Carolina, led to a GM position with the Gastonia Grizzlies. At twenty-three, and with no prior experience, I was in charge of turning their failed fortunes around.

Faced with such a massive undertaking, I eventually found my yellow tux.

Okay, so it was a black tux at first. One of my buddies owned a bridal and formal shop, and he set me up in a nice black-and-white number, complete with tails that practically swept the ground. I felt just like P.T. Barnum.

Then I remembered I lived in the South, where a black tux and hundred-degree weather went together about as well as toothpaste and orange juice. After melting into a puddle that first night, I decided I needed something else.

One trip to brightcoloredtuxedos.com later, and I was the Yellow Tux Guy. These days, I couldn't take that tux off even if I wanted to. Fans love it, and my staff says it helps them know where I am at all times. I'm the most visible guy in the ballpark, and that's just fine with me.

Being the Yellow Tux Guy brings me a lot of attention. But

at the end of the day, it's not about me. It's about having fun and doing something different. It's about inspiring others to live better lives than the ones they've been told to live.

Above all, it's about the fans, the community, and creating the best experience possible.

WHY THIS BOOK?

I feel incredibly fortunate for the world we've created with Fans First Entertainment. However, I don't want to keep this feeling all to myself. I found *my* yellow tux, and now I want you to find *yours*.

That's what this book is all about.

WHAT DOES FINDING YOUR YELLOW TUX MEAN?

First, I should clarify that I don't mean this literally. Unless you really, really want to, there's no need to put on an actual yellow tux of your own.

Instead, finding your yellow tux is about standing out and sharing the best version of yourself.

It's about you, your business, and your legacy.

It's about living your life turned up to ten.

It's about amplifying your message, sharing it with anyone who will listen, and leaving a lasting impact on the world.

That's how the best business leaders are made. *That's* what I'm going to help you become.

Ultimately, the business you create is your choice. You can keep doing your thing day in and day out, or you can commit to making a real impact. You can keep waking up at the same time every day, sitting through the same traffic, and running your staff through the same routines. Or, you can commit to finding your yellow tux, to bringing passion and excitement to the workplace, and to inspiring your staff, fans, and community in the process.

Your call.

STOP STANDING STILL, START STANDING OUT

In almost every corner of life—whether colleges, factories, or corporate offices—people are in a mad rush to the middle. We're applauded for showing up on time, going about our business, and otherwise fitting in.

Perhaps you're fine with that. Perhaps all you want to do

is go about your day and do your thing. But here's the problem: *you're not doing your thing.* You're doing someone else's thing. You're doing what's expected of you.

That's why I say if it's normal, do the exact opposite.

Normal will get you through the day, but it's not fulfilling. In fact, fitting in is hard. Fitting in impacts all kinds of daily choices. It affects the clothes you wear, the shows you watch, and the jobs you take.

Unfortunately, it doesn't do any one of us a lick of good. In fact, it's probably doing us a lot of harm. Sure, it may bring you a steady paycheck, but it also leads to a lot of stress and anxiety.

The truth is you'll find more success and happiness by being yourself. *That's* what finding your yellow tux is all about.

YELLOW TUXING ISN'T RANDOM

With that out of the way, let's get one thing clear: yellow tuxing isn't about being different for the sake of being different. I could have been different by writing this book in hieroglyphics, but it wouldn't have helped me share my message with you any better.

I'm not asking you to be anyone other than who you are. Instead, I'm challenging you to become the *best version* of who you are. I want you to remember why you got into business in the first place. I want you to come home from work every day feeling fulfilled, like you've contributed to something special. I want people to remember you for the difference you made in their lives.

My life has taught me that when you embrace the outrageous, the ridiculous, and the fun, you become a better business owner. Why? Because you're creating a business that reflects *who you are*.

When you commit to fun, everyone else around you has fun too. When they have fun, they do better work. When they do better work, your company grows and succeeds. That's the payoff of this book, and in the following chapters, I'll show you how it's done.

HOW TO READ THIS BOOK

Okay, we're almost ready to set out on our journey. But first, some notes on how I've set things up.

THE THREE-PRONGED APPROACH

I've designed this book to be a fun read with easy, practical lessons. To that end, I've divided it into three parts:

- Part I: Yellow Tuxing Yourself
- Part II: Yellow Tuxing Your Business
- Part III: Yellow Tuxing Your Legacy

Throughout this book, you're going to learn my story and how I came to find my yellow tux. You're also going to learn the stories of those who inspired me, entrepreneurs and mentors like Walt Disney, P.T. Barnum, and Bill Veeck. Fans First Entertainment wouldn't be what it is today without their leadership, and I'm sure their stories will inspire you the same way they inspired me.

QUESTIONS, QUESTIONS, QUESTIONS

This book is about you. It's about self-realization. It's about learning how to be successful by standing out.

I've included questions at the end of every chapter to help you reach that goal. After all, in order to get where you want to go, first you have to know where you are.

These questions aren't just an exercise for fun. They're an important part of the process. They will help you determine whether you're ready to stand out in your business and stand out in your life.

So in that spirit, make sure to answer every question and add up your scores. At the end of the book, I promise there will be a payoff.

Let's get started with your first set of questions right now.

THE YELLOW TUXOMETER

For each question, answer with one of the following: all the time (ten points), sometimes (five points), or never (one point).

1. Do you plan and set up events for you and your friends?

2. How often do you initiate conversations with strangers?

3. Would your friends or spouse describe you as a go-getter?

THE YELLOW TUX BOOKSHELF

Because you can never learn too much, I'm also going to share some of my favorite books with you at the end of every chapter.

These books—and many others—have been an invaluable resource for me as a business owner. The truth is, I didn't enjoy reading in school. It would have helped a lot, but nope, I'd decided it wasn't for me.

That all changed once I became the GM of the Gastonia Grizzlies. If I was going to fix a failing team, I needed to learn a lot and learn it fast. Ever since then, I've been reading several books a week, and I've never looked back.

I do have one request though. Don't keep all this knowledge to yourself. Just as I'm sharing these books with you, I encourage you to share them with others—especially your employees.

Here's why. In the book *Worth Doing Wrong*, author Arnie Malham, shares how he started a book club at his advertising agency in Nashville, Tennessee. He would pay his employees to read—$25, $50, $75, sometimes even $100 a book. Not only did he see a dramatic improvement in both employee culture and performance, but he also got to watch his employees fall in love with reading just like he had.

Arnie's Better Book Club grew from there. Seven years later, he has invested almost $100,000 in his employees through this reading program. In fact, it became such an important part of his business that he began introducing the concept to other companies.

Today, companies from all over the world are part of the Better Book Club, including my company, Fans First Entertainment. In our first year of implementing it in 2017, this book club has helped our employees continue to grow and be hungry every day.

That's why I'm sharing the Yellow Tux Bookshelf with you. I've been fortunate to get to know a lot of these authors and they continue to inspire me every day. I hope they can share some inspiration with you.

OH, THERE ARE VIDEOS AND MUSIC TOO

We love sharing our antics, and this book wouldn't be complete if I didn't share some of those antics with you— as well as a few choice music recommendations. To get the full Fans First Experience (or, at least the full Fans First Experience we can offer in book form), check the footnotes and follow the links to get a better sense of what we're all about.

LET'S GO BANANAS

As you move through the following chapters, keep in mind

this isn't a book about making more money or improving workplace productivity. It's a book about making yourself happier with the work you do, about embracing your passion, and about building a better business—a business that represents *you*.

If you can do that, then the money and success will follow. But first, to build a better business, you have to build a better self.

All set? Good. It's time to stop standing still and start standing out.

Part 1

YELLOW TUXING
YOURSELF

CHAPTER *One*

THE MIRROR MOMENT

The first step to becoming an entrepreneur does not happen in a laboratory, a conference room, or even a pitch session. It happens in the mind. It happens in the place where you start to get worried about your rent, your mortgage, your children, your debt building up on your credit card. It happens when you are exposed.

—LINDA ROTTENBERG, CRAZY IS A COMPLIMENT

In the opening scene of *Jerry Maguire*, Tom Cruise's title character is teetering on the edge between breakthrough and breakdown.

Up to this point, his whole life has revolved around landing star athletes, negotiating blockbuster deals, and riding the gravy train. By most measures, he's a success, but he still isn't happy.

Something has to change. So, he sits down to write a new mission statement for his company. And as his mission statement grows, so does his inspiration. He gets manic, bouncing around his home and doing handstands, but always returning back to the warm, inviting glow of his computer.

Suddenly, he's remembering the simple pleasures of his job, the way he came to his profession out of law school, and the way the stadium sounds when one of his players performs well on the field. "A night like this doesn't come along very often," he says. "I seized it."

It all made sense now; his company was too concerned with money and taking too many clients. As Cruise says in the voiceover, "With so many clients, we had forgotten what was important." His solution? Fewer clients, less money.

After distributing the memo, he's greeted with a standing ovation—and then promptly fired. The movie takes off from there with Jerry fighting the good fight for his sole, remaining client. And because it's Hollywood, his grand vision eventually pays off.

Jerry's all-night writing session set the tone for the entire movie. With that scene, we understand that character instantly, because we understand his fundamental frustration.

That's what mirror moments—the first step in our journey—are all about.

However, to get that initial spark, first, we need a catalyst.

WHAT IS A MIRROR MOMENT, ANYWAY?

There's a key difference between Jerry Maguire and most other entrepreneurs. While he took a big risk and acted on his mirror moment, the rest of us are content to bite our tongues and keep our frustrations inside.

Now, I'm not suggesting that you distribute revolutionary business memos in your office. If you're still an aspiring business leader, I'd hate to be the reason you get fired from your job.

However, I *am* suggesting that when something bothers you about your work, you take notice and *do something about it*. Mirror moments allow you to look at what you're doing, ask whether it's right, whether you believe in what you're doing, and whether you could be doing it better.

IT BEGINS WITH A CHALLENGE

If you don't care about being different in your industry and finding a better solution, you are in the wrong job. It's time to move on to something else.

That's how it was for me anyway. The entrepreneurial light first switched on right after college, when my father offered me a coaching job at his business, the South Shore Baseball Club.

It was a good offer, but something didn't feel right. After a couple of trials and errors, I realized I didn't want to become a coach. I wanted to carve my own path instead. So, I committed to running the Gastonia Grizzlies, a ball club on the brink of failure and with no obvious path to success.

This was the first of many professional mirror moments for me. Through it, I learned that no matter who we are, we all have to take a step back and take stock of ourselves. Often, it's the only way to move forward.

THE BEGINNING OF SOMETHING BETTER

I'm not one for negativity. I'd rather focus on finding a fun solution than dwell on a problem. Trust me, the irony is not lost on me that the first chapter of this book is all about focusing on your problems.

Just think of it as a starting point. For any business to move forward, you have to figure out what's holding you back. That means asking yourself:

- What frustrates you about your business?
- What frustrates your customers?
- What do people say when they complain about your industry, and what do they mean when they say it?

I don't ignore more problems. I just see them a little differently. Where some might see a problem as a brick wall, I see it as fuel for the idea machine.

A good entrepreneur asks these questions constantly. As soon as you know what you don't like, you can start thinking about what you'd rather do instead. And once you know that, you're free to start doing your own thing.

When I first became GM of Gastonia, our problems were many and obvious. We had no money. No one wanted to sponsor us. No one even knew who we were. I was lucky in a sense. It was obvious what I needed to do.

Some businesses—even entire industries—aren't so lucky. They can ignore deep, underlying issues and coast on past successes for years. Blockbuster was happy to maintain the status quo until Netflix came around. So was the hotel industry before Airbnb popped up.

Mirror moments allow us to confront lingering issues and reinvent ourselves before it's too late. They're not about dwelling on the negatives. They're about starting off on the right foot by facing any negativity, pushing through it, and creating something better.

COMMITTING TO GROWTH

At Fans First Entertainment, we have what we call the "Fans First Way," which states, "Always Be Caring, Different, Enthusiastic, Fun, Growing, and Hungry."

I tend to put a special emphasis on the last two. I want the same thing for my employees as I want for myself—to be growing and hungry. I want them to stare challenges right in the face, find a solution, and build off the experience.

To keep growing and being hungry, you need two things: self-awareness and a willingness to fail. This means being able to look at yourself and say, "You know what? I'm not good at this, and I'm hurting my business because of it." If you can get to that level of honesty with yourself, that's when the real fun begins.

I certainly learned this with the Grizzlies. My first year, I did a little bit of everything—working concessions, ordering merchandise, and even helping with the player roster.

Actually, I didn't just help with the roster. I wanted so badly to be part of a winning team that I took it upon myself to do all the recruiting. I figured since I loved baseball and had played it my whole life, I had to know something about putting a team together. That makes sense, right?

Wrong. We opened the season 0-7.

Enter another mirror moment. I realized I wasn't in the baseball circles anymore, recruiting was not my strength, and I had no business doing it. After admitting that, I was happy to let the coaches take over and work their magic.

I'd love to say that I learned my lesson, that I've never gotten in my business' way since, but I'd be lying if I did. Instead, I'll offer these two words: zip ties.

I *suck* at zip ties. It takes me thirty minutes to put up a sign that someone else could put up in five. Really, it's not just zip ties. I'm basically a human roadblock when it comes to any sort of operational task like that.

Luckily, my staff has learned to laugh at my superhuman

lack of skills. Whenever they see me struggling with a zip tie or something similar, they just laugh and say, "Jesse, you're slowing us all down again. Get out of the way!" If nothing else, at least we can all make a joke out of it. They've even started calling me "Jesse Ops" to make a joke out of how much I suck at operations.

FAIL FORWARD

The mirror moment isn't a one-and-done thing. It's a process.

Nothing wrong with that. A commitment to growth is the Fans First Way. It doesn't matter if you get things right the first day you try—or ever, for that matter. As we'll discuss more in the next chapter, sometimes the solution is to let someone else take over.

Take a day in my life, for example. I know it's my job to put on a show, to be the Yellow Tux Guy. I *know* this, and yet it still takes every ounce of strength I have not to jump into the concessions stand and try to help out when I see a long line.

The truth is I wouldn't be any help anyway. I'd just get in the way of the people who know what they're doing. Worse, I'd be ignoring my own responsibility to the show.

I bet you have a figurative concession stand at your business too. I bet that some days, even when you know better, you can't help but jump in.

Don't beat yourself up over it when you do. How else are you going to know unless you fail a few times first?

FIGHTING FIREFIGHTER FATIGUE

Rather than president, owner, or CEO, the title most business people and entrepreneurs should have is firefighter. When I'm out there with the zip ties or at the concession stand, I'm not making the best use of my time. I'm not helping my business. I'm putting out fires—and not very well!

Playing firefighter is neither fulfilling nor sustainable. But being proactive is. Every day, every week, use mirror moments to think about both the things your business isn't great at and the things you're not great at in your business. Then, instead of throwing yourself into the fire to try and rescue everyone all the time, try thinking about how your team can avoid starting the fire in the first place.

BALANCING THE INTERNAL AND EXTERNAL

Your business is an extension of you. That means it's going

to reflect both your strengths and your weaknesses. By focusing on internal mirror moments first, you make it more likely that your business reflects *the best* of you, and not some fun-house version of yourself.

Here's what I mean. Like many entrepreneurs, I've lived quite the roller-coaster life the past decade. Some days, I'm a walking ball of anxiety. Other days, I'm floating around worry-free.

Through mirror moments, I've learned that I'm most stressed when I'm not playing to my strengths. Instead, I'm out playing firefighter, tying zip ties, or working in the concessions stand.

When I stick to the things I love, everything is different. Get me in a room with Ben, our videographer, where we're laughing about our Batman-inspired video for "Batboy," and I couldn't be happier. Get me thinking about some operational problem that I don't know how to solve, and watch as the wheels start to come off.

It took some work for me to figure this out. But in the process, I realized how valuable it was to turn the mirror on myself first before turning it on my business.

CLOCK WATCHING

When you're at work, do you watch the clock, or do you lose track of time?

With our teams, none of us know what day it is at our office. Sure, we know when it's game day and what promotion we're running, but otherwise, we're always losing track of time.

This isn't because we're lazy. We work long, long days at our ballparks. A lot of time and effort goes into putting on one of our shows. And yet, once the crowds have departed and we've cleaned everything up, no one wants to leave. Sometimes we stick around until one in the morning or later, talking about the day, learning from each other, and celebrating what we've accomplished.

I've learned that when you're working for something bigger than yourself, the hours don't matter. My employees lose track of time because they're having so much fun. As I like to say, if you're not laughing like a hyena every day at work—if you're not doubled over with tears in your eyes gasping for breath as you try to process the ridiculous thing that just happened—then you're missing something.

BUSY IS NOT A BADGE OF HONOR

People love to talk about how busy they are. Sometimes it's to complain. Sometimes it's to show off how important they are.

But why? It's not like they're going to get an award for being busy—especially if they're not actually getting anything done.

At Fans First, we may work hard, but we never tell people we are busy.

Instead, we show up when we need to, we work hard, and we go home when the job is done. Actually, sometimes we just stick around and play kickball for a few hours. *Then* we go home.

The point is, if you tell others you're living the dream, make sure you actually are. Forget the meetings you don't need to attend, the fires you don't need to put out, and the tasks you aren't any good at anyway.

Instead, fill your day with purpose and passion. Stop watching the clock, and start having fun.

FIND YOUR TWO-WAY MIRRORS

Sometimes it takes the insights of others to help you take a look at yourself and figure out a path forward. That's where the best mentors come in. Here are a couple of mirror moments that stood out to me.

EMBRACING THE CIRCUS

In 2007, I became GM of a failing ball club (more on that in the next chapter). Faced with a make-or-break situation, I had no choice but to take stock of what we were doing and figure out a path forward. Being a baseball team was not working. I loved the sport, but even I knew the Grizzlies were flat-out boring at the time.

The only way to change that was to bring the city of Gastonia something they had never seen. And after a lot of soul-searching, reading, and learning from others, I had my solution; we were going to become a circus—a baseball circus, but a circus nonetheless.

Now all I had to do was recruit the team's owner, Ken Silver, into my vision.

Ken could have fired me on the spot. Instead, he let me run with it. He saw that I'd given the matter a lot of thought, he saw my enthusiasm, and he chose to believe in me, mentoring and guiding me where he could.

The great thing about Ken is that he rarely gave me the advice I was looking for. He was the perfect two-way mirror. He saw what I was doing and reflected it back at me.

Whenever I'd approached him with some crazy idea—say, a five-hundred-person pillow fight in the middle of the field—he would just look at me, smile, and say, "What do you think?"

Somehow, those simple words always managed to put any idea in perspective.

When I took over as owner of the Grizzlies, I promised to pay Ken's mentorship forward. Now, whenever an employee comes up to me looking for advice, I let Ken do the talking and just say, "What do you think?"

TAKE A LOOK AT YOURSELF AND MAKE THE CHANGE

Hal Elrod changed my mornings. Actually, with his book, *Miracle Morning*, he changed a lot of people's mornings.

HYPE MUSIC

I was obsessed with Michael Jackson when I was a kid.
I'd listen to his music nonstop. I even learned how to
moonwalk (kinda).

That's why, before you start reading the following section, you have to put on the Gloved One's "Man in the
Mirror" and have yourself a good time (YouTube keywords: "Michael Jackson Man in the Mirror").

As Hal explains, he almost died twice—once literally in a car accident, and once mentally during a particularly rough patch in his life.

At the time, Hal had lost everything, and suicidal thoughts began to creep in. He took one look at himself and realized that if something didn't change, his life was literally in danger.

To save his life, he came up with the concept of Life SAVERS. Here, the SAVERS acronym stands for Silence, Affirmation, Visualization, Exercise, Reading, and Scribing. Driving this concept was his desire to be more appreciative of life and to celebrate gratitude.

Everything changed when Hal Elrod put his Life SAVERS

concept into practice. He became a new person. He tripled his revenue. He became a better husband and father. In all facets of life, he was winning.

Hal changed when he realized that while most people run on autopilot in the morning, most *successful people* start their day intentionally.

After reading his book, I realized I fell into the former camp. Every day, I'd wake up, look at my phone, and scroll through Facebook. Then I would eat cereal, watch *SportsCenter*, check and respond to emails, and head into work.

By the time I got to work every day, I was in a bad mood. I didn't know why until I read *Miracle Morning*. Afterward, it all seemed obvious; I wasn't starting my day on purpose. Instead, I let others start my day—people on Facebook, people sending emails, people on TV. I was forced to think and respond to them, rather than start the day on my own terms.

As Hal puts it, "Win the morning, win the day." I've modeled my mornings off of these words. My mornings are *on purpose*, and I bring this sense of purpose to my staff every day when I walk in the door.

All throughout this chapter, I've encouraged you to ask

some tough questions. I've told you to take a look at what you suck at and what your business sucks at. I've told you to take a look at the things you hate about your job and what stresses you out—even simple things like distracting yourself with the phone in the morning.

This isn't because I want you to start running around declaring how bad you feel or how terrible both you and everyone else around you are doing.

After all, I'm the Yellow Tux Guy. I'm not trying to put any more negativity in the world (especially not on Facebook for you to see first thing in the morning).

But here's the thing: when you know you suck at something, or when you know you're unhappy, that's the best possible place to be. From there, you can actually start to do something about it.

Ultimately, that's what the mirror moment is all about—fulfillment.

As we'll discuss in the next chapter, businesses thrive when their leaders are able to not only identify their strengths, but also create an environment where they can flourish. The process involves some trial and error—there will be some things you don't yet know you're good at, and other things you *think* you're good at but aren't—but the results will transform the way you solve problems and generate ideas.

THE YELLOW TUXOMETER

For each question, provide one of the following responses: all the time (ten points), sometimes (five points), or never (one point).

1. How often do you come home from work feeling energized?

2. Do you want your spouse and kids to ask you about your day at work?

3. Do you talk proudly to others about the work you are doing?

THE YELLOW TUX BOOKSHELF

Read on, reader! The business leaders with the yellowest of yellow tuxes all know how to stop and take a long look in the mirror every once in a while. If you want to take your self-reflection skills a little further, check out the following books.

- *Miracle Morning*, by Hal Elrod

- *Start with Why*, by Simon Sinek

- *Ego Is the Enemy*, by Ryan Holiday

- *Anything You Want*, by Derek Sivers

- *Peak*, by Chip Conley

- *Success Is a Decision*, by Tim Connor

CHAPTER *Two*

THE BEST QUESTION

Finding your passion isn't just about careers and money. It's about finding your authentic self. The one you've buried underneath people's needs.

—KRISTIN HANNAH

Jiro Ono is the best sushi chef in the world.

Everything he does is practiced, precise, and *his way*. He only serves ten people at a time, charging about 30,000 yen (or $281) for a tasting. No appetizers, no frills. He serves guests what he wants and in the best way he knows how.

No one tells Jiro Ono how to do his job. He follows what he believes, and he holds his beliefs with a fierce passion.

To him, the secret to success is determining what you're

best at and committing to it fully. As he says in the documentary *Jiro Dreams of Sushi*, "You have to fall in love with your work and never complain about your job. You must dedicate your life to mastering the skill."

Talent got Jiro started, but dedication to his craft got him the rest of the way. He follows the same routine every day. He tastes every piece of sushi before it goes out. He's obsessed with the texture of his food.

I'm a big fan of Jiro Ono.[9] Really, there's a lot to like, but for our purposes, it comes down to two things: Jiro knows what he's best at, and he pursues that talent with a passion.

WHAT ARE YOU BEST AT?

Choosing what you're best at over other considerations isn't easy. It takes a belief in yourself and a willingness to walk a different path that a lot of people haven't.

If you follow this path, it could mean leaving behind a comfortable lifestyle. It could mean struggling to bring home a paycheck, food, or little surprises for the family. But it also could mean a more effective and fulfilling business.

---

9   If you watch *Jiro Dreams of Sushi* on Netflix, you'll be a fan too!

AMPLIFY YOU

I'm loud. I'm outspoken. I'm over the top.

I've been called Crazy and names I can't even share. You name it. I've heard a lot over the years.

It bothered me at first. A lot. Then I realized something: they were right. That's me.

I'm not quiet or reserved. In fact, I hate holding back. I love sharing crazy ideas and pushing the envelope with everything I do.

Sure, it hurts sometimes when you throw yourself out there and don't get the response you were hoping for. I don't like that feeling any more than you do. I understand the impulse to conform and try to be like everyone else.

The thing is, it's not going to get you anywhere. So here's what I say: Amplify yourself. Go deep on your strengths. Instead of worrying about being well-rounded, take a tip from Jiro and focus on being the best at one thing.

That means if you're an amazing singer, then sing. Sing often, sing loud, sing proud. Someone will see the value in what you do. Heck, it could be me. One of my dreams is to hire a team of amazing singers to work our concession stands.

Naturally, there are plenty of other places you can sing. The other day, I was watching YouTube videos of a singing dentist. Whenever this guy is hard at work on someone's teeth, he's singing Ed Sheeran or Katy Perry, acting about as ridiculous as he can while still getting the job done.

I guarantee you more people would rather visit a singing dentist than a by-the-book stiff who barely says anything as they poke and prod away and tell you how badly you need to start flossing. I know I'd like him for *my* dentist.

The point is, you can amplify yourself and still be good at your job. In my experience, most of us actually do *better* when we allow ourselves to cut loose, have fun, and create an environment that reflects *who we are*.

This doesn't mean you won't get criticized. As a wise person once said, "haters gonna hate." But it's better to get called a few names than to give up the thing you're best at.

WHAT'S MOST WORTH YOUR TIME?

There isn't enough time in the world to be phenomenal at everything. If becoming a well-rounded human being is on your bucket list, all the power to you. However, you'll get there a lot faster if you triple down on your personal strengths, rather than spend all your time trying to get a tiny bit better at one of your weaknesses.

THE SATURDAY MORNING TEST

Some will put years of hard work and education into what they *think* they're best at. Others will force themselves to be best at something because of the paycheck or accreditation.

If you fall into that category, then what you're best at *right now* may not be what you're *actually* the best at.

In *The Happiness Equation,* author Neil Pasricha introduces the Saturday Morning Test. It's beautiful in its simplicity. All you have to do is ask yourself what's your favorite thing to do on a Saturday morning when you've got nothing else going on? What are your hobbies and side hustles?

Maybe you make delicious brunches. Maybe you like working on your car. Maybe you garden. Maybe you scour antique shops for strange treasures. Maybe you ride horses. Maybe you draw elaborate pictures on golf balls with Sharpies.

Whatever it is, it's at least related to the thing you're best at.

The question is, how can you bring that talent to your business—or better yet, how can you make it your business?

THE HOST WITH THE MOST?

In Gastonia, I had plenty of reasons to think I would make a good on-field host. I was the Yellow Tux Guy, after all. I was in charge of leading promotions, bringing the energy, and putting on the show. I was good at all these things. In fact, I consider them some of my greatest strengths.

After a while, however, I realized that being the on-field host was a little different. I was okay at it, but I needed someone better, someone quick on their feet who always knew what to say.

SEEKING THAT SPECIAL SOMEONE

We searched different colleges, improv and theater departments, trying to find the right personality to lead the on-field circus. Unfortunately, no one in the theater world wanted anything to do with a lowly baseball team.

Finally, I discovered there was a local college, Queens University, up in Charlotte—less than thirty minutes from Gastonia. We reached out to the president of their improv group for a phone interview, and he said, "Yeah, I'd love to have an interview and talk about it."

He was outstanding.

At the end of the interview, we said, "Why don't you just come over for an actual audition at the ballpark? If we can schedule something in the next few days, you can just drive down here and do your thing."

He answered, "I can't do that."

"What do you mean?" we asked.

"This is Queens University in Ontario, Canada. This isn't Queens in Charlotte."

Add "looking up the right university" to my list of things I'm not best at.

That said, we weren't fond of the word "can't." So, months after going through the visa application and a Canadian Mountie costume later, we got our man to Gastonia—and he was everything we could've ever imagined.

WHO'S BETTER THAN YOU?

It's important to surround yourself with people who are better than you at something. Sometimes they'll save you from doing something you hate, and sometimes they'll improve upon something you like. Either way, by letting yourself take a step back, you allow your business to take a step forward.

In other words, it's better to have several phenomenal people than a few well-rounded ones. The more you can bring in people to do what they do best, the more you free yourself to do the same.

IF YOU'RE BORED, DO SOMETHING ELSE

In the last chapter, I mentioned I had a pretty rough landing coming into Gastonia. Here's how bad it really was.

My first day in the office, my head just about fell off. With every new bit of information I uncovered, the picture got even bleaker. The Grizzlies were averaging only a couple hundred fans a game and losing over $150,000 a year. Even worse, we had only a couple hundred dollars left in the bank, and I had to figure out how to pay my three full-time staff members by Friday.

The money had to come from somewhere. So, I started

making phone calls to try and bring in some sponsors. No one cared. Even after seven years in the city, no one even knew who we were. The rare businesses that did know us either refused to work with us or hung up before I could even ask.

There was no sense dressing it up. Being a baseball team was not working. We were so boring, we couldn't even draw flies.

As I saw it, the only way to change that was to bring the city of Gastonia something they had never seen before.

There was only one thing stopping me; I had no idea what that meant.

WHAT COULD WE BE BEST AT?

Eager for an answer, I started reading as many books and attended as many conferences as I could. I was especially moved by the works of Bill Veeck, who had owned several ball clubs throughout the twentieth century. So, when I saw that his son, Mike, was hosting his own conference, I leapt at the opportunity to meet him.

Mike was as warm, intelligent, and helpful as I'd hoped. He listened to my problems, saw the sincerity and desperation in my eyes, and said, "One, you've got to be the face of the team. And two, you've got to get a little crazy."

That advice changed my life.

After meeting with Mike, I read about P.T. Barnum and Walt Disney, focusing on the experiences they created for their fans and visitors. I wanted to create a similar experience at Grizzlies games. But first, I had to convince our owner, Ken, and just about everyone else.

BUILDING BUY-IN

Once I got him on the phone, I said, "Ken, we're no longer going to be a baseball team. We're going to be all about entertainment."

He could have hung up on me right there, but he knew he had nothing to lose by hearing me out. "What do you have in mind?" he said.

"Our players are going to do choreographed dances," I replied. "We're going to have grandma beauty pageants. I'm getting dunked in the dunk tank every game. We're going to serve burgers inside donut buns. We're going to build a circus."

With Ken's blessing, I set my vision in motion. Our first task was to train our players to dance.

For the first practice, I hired a choreographer to come out and show the players some moves. But just as she was taking them through the steps of Apaches's classic, "Jump on It," one of the guys stopped, threw his arms up in the air, and said, "I'm not doing this."

Fair enough. We didn't force the issue.

A few games later, he was singing a different tune. The Jump-on-It dancers had become the most popular players on the team, and he decided he wanted in on the action.

Suddenly, he was the best, most active dancer we had. He'd rip his belt off and swing it over his head. He'd sing Backstreet Boys during "Grizzly Idol" night. He'd do whatever it took to get the crowd into it—even if it meant ripping off his jersey. A few years later, I found out he'd become a male model after seeing pictures of his billboards on Facebook.

Sure enough, he found what he was best at. But more importantly, he showed us all how far we could go by committing ourselves fully to being entertainers.

From there, things grew. We tried a lot of things. Some worked, and some didn't (Salute to Underwear Night? Yeah, that one didn't pan out). Regardless, our reputation grew, and even people who hated baseball showed up for our games.

In fact, hating baseball became one of our selling points. For every potential visitor who told me they hated baseball, I replied, "Perfect! You'll love our show!" Everyone still saw us as a baseball team, but we knew what business we were *really* in.

In the process, I realized I'd always been an entertainer. It's what I was best at. One of my favorite things about my days as a pitcher was that I could control the game. For better or worse, it was *my* show.

With the Grizzlies, I couldn't control what happened on the field. However, I could still control the show. It was my job to create an exceptional fan experience by celebrating them, encouraging them to participate, and making them feel welcome no matter what. That became the core of what Fans First Entertainment is all about.

IT TAKES A WHILE TO REALIZE WHAT YOU'RE BEST AT

Most of my life, I thought I was best at baseball. After blowing out my arm in college, that was no longer an option. I figured if I couldn't be best at baseball, I could be best at coaching.

After graduating college, I interned with the Spartanburg Stingers in the spring and committed to joining the Gastonia Grizzlies as GM in the fall. In the meantime, I went to coach in the Cape Cod League, one of the most well-known college summer leagues in the country.

As the volunteer assistant coach, I couldn't be any lower on the totem pole than I was. I had few actual responsibilities, zero say in any coaching decisions, and zero room for creativity. My days were spent performing odd jobs and helping where I could on the field. I did fine, but I knew something was missing.

One day, after a particularly cold summer night, we were warming up on the field. Since I was a coach, I decided I needed to sound like a coach. So, I looked at the team and said the coachiest thing I could think of, "Make sure you stretch. You don't want to pull any hamstrings."

No one said a thing, but I could tell from their faces they were all thinking, "Who *is* this guy?"

Later on in the dugout, I had myself a little mirror moment. There I was, occupying the best seat in the house, surrounded by the best collegiate players in the country, participating in a sport I had played and loved my entire life—and I was so miserable.

I would count down the hours until the games, and then, I would count down the innings until I could go home. No one cared that I was there, including myself.

It was obvious I wasn't doing what I was best at. That night, I resolved to never feel that way again.

UNCLE WALT

When I tried coaching, I thought I knew what I wanted, but it turned out I was wrong. Coaching simply didn't excite me. When I finally accepted that, I was able to pivot and dive into what I was good at—entertainment.

It can be hard to make the switch from good to great, especially if it means leaving behind what you're used to. However, if what you're used to doesn't excite you, if it doesn't make you leap out of bed every day, then perhaps it's time to ask yourself the best question.

But don't take it from me. Take it from Uncle Walt.

One of my greatest mentors is Walt Disney. To the world, he's remembered as a master animator, producer, engineer, and designer.

Walt, however, knew he wasn't the best at any of those things. In fact, he fired himself from various roles repeatedly throughout his career and replaced himself with others who were ten times better than he was. Why? So he could focus on the part of his company that he knew he was best at: being a visionary.

Disney enjoyed selling his vision to others and put all his energy into that goal. And he wasn't aloof about it either. He would act out entire scenes for his staff until they shared his vision. He would even inspect his animators' desks for their best work at the end of every day.

Once the animators figured this out, they began to leave what they considered their best work on top of their desk every night.

Disney had a different idea of what "best" meant, however.

To make sure every movie lived up to his vision, he would often sort through the animators' waste bins, carefully selecting his favorite works and putting them back on the animators' desks.

It didn't matter if someone else thought it was trash. If Uncle Walt loved it, that was the end of that.

Not only did he have the good judgment to do what he was great at, but he also had the courage to blaze his own trail. Walt wasn't held back by what Gay Hendricks calls the "upper limit problem," or the idea that we impose our own glass ceiling as a way of sabotaging our own success. Once he found his zone of genius, he never left.

You can't create everything yourself. However, you *can* have a vision, and you can share it passionately with others, and they can help you build it. Every great thing in life has been inspired by one, but accomplished by many.

We live by this philosophy at our ballparks. I may be able to see exactly how a promotion should go to get people laughing and having fun, but I know I can't pull it off myself. I need to make sure I have the actors, the performers, and the props. I need to have the fans in the right place. That's what I'm best at: orchestrating, promoting, and making all the pieces fit.

Sometimes this means swapping out indifferent contestants for more energetic participants at the last minute just to make sure an on-field promotion is actually entertaining. Other times, it means trusting my performers to keep things fun when a promotion goes wrong—usually by embracing the failure and making it part of the show.

When you've figured out what you're best at, when you've surrounded yourself with people who know what *they're* best at, it's easy to roll with whatever comes your way.

So how about it? What are you best at?

THE YELLOW TUXOMETER

For each question, answer with one of the following: all the time (ten points), sometimes (five points), or never (one point).

1. How often do you do things at work that you don't enjoy?

2. Do you surround yourself with people more successful than you?

3. Do you lose track of time at work?

THE YELLOW TUX BOOKSHELF

You wanted the best, you got the best—the best books on becoming the best version of yourself, that is.

- *Be the Best at What Matters Most*, by Joe Calloway

- *Happiness Equation*, by Neil Pasrichia

- *The Success Intersection*, by Pat Williams

- *Choose Yourself*, by James Altucher

- *Happiness Advantage*, by Shawn Achor

- *48 Days to the Work You Love*, by Dan Miller

- *Strengths Finder 2.0, by Tom Rath*

CHAPTER *Three*

BE A SPONGE

Anyone who stops learning is old, whether at twenty or eighty. Anyone who keeps learning is young.

—HENRY FORD

My biggest fear in life is settling. This fear drives me to work harder every second of every day. I need to keep growing, learning, succeeding, and pushing myself. It doesn't matter if I reach my goal, or even if I achieve something great.

Sure, I'll celebrate my successes, but afterward, I try not to rest on my laurels. I want to go further and be more. In my business, I have a huge responsibility to my community, to my fans, and to my staff. To take care of them, I need to keep growing.

So, I am a sponge.

I walk around the field with a book in hand, immersing myself in ideas and approaches to make myself and my business better. I want to learn everything I can—and I want my staff to also.

The way I see it, it's the only way to build on past successes and keep pushing for something greater.

SUPER ABSORBENT

Being a sponge means opening your mind to new ideas and possibilities. It means listening to others rather than clinging to your old knowledge and bad habits. It means taking insights from a new, different area of wisdom—a sector maybe parallel or adjacent to your own.

Sponges absorb. That's what they do, and they're very good at it. When you're a sponge, you start out dry. Next, you start soaking up the world around you and learning new things. And after all that, you take everything you've soaked up and start applying that knowledge in new and exciting ways.

THE VOICE IN YOUR HEAD

I'm fueled by the urge to make my work special, meaningful, and impactful. It's all that little voice in my head whispers in my ear day and night.

Your inner voice may be saying something completely different. That's fine. Give it a listen. Whatever it's saying, that's your starting point to becoming a sponge. That's the thing you need to learn and how you can go about doing it.

EXTERNAL FORCES

Through that lens, seek out your external forces. Who inspires you? How did they push the limits of their own greatness, and how can you apply that to your own life?

These external forces can be a cherished mentor—like Walt Disney, P. T. Barnum, or Bill Veeck for me—or someone in your everyday life. Your external forces don't even have to be positive or uplifting. They just need to motivate you.

INTERNAL + EXTERNAL = FEEDBACK LOOP

I'll give you an example. When I was a child, I worked hard to bring the best grades home to my father. Usually I was an A student, so if an A-minus found its way onto my report card, he was sure to notice.

"What happened with the A-minus?" he would ask. Today I know that he was joking, that he was always proud of the work I did no matter what. However, I wasn't always sure of that back then, and that gentle ribbing helped hardwire me to do my best.

Here's where things get tricky. I'm grateful for both the internal and external forces that push me forward to do my best. However, I realize those same forces can conspire to keep me stuck in old ways of thinking.

A sponge that gets stuck in old patterns stops absorbing. When a sponge stops absorbing, it slowly dries out. And, well, a dry sponge kinda stinks.

No one lives up to their own standards all the time. I didn't when I brought home the occasional A-minus, and I don't on the nights I don't put on the best show I can for my fans.

Usually in these off moments, I would feel like I deserved some sort of punishment. Actually, if I'm being honest, I still feel that way sometimes.

For instance, in Gastonia, we had games where we only had five hundred people come to the ballpark. By the standards we've set, that's a pretty lousy Tuesday night.

It still bothers me now, but it would have eaten away at me before. Literally, I would have been sick inside wondering what people thought of me. Here I was, the Yellow Tux

Guy, talking about all his success, and I could barely get five hundred people to come to our show.

Now I realize that one night isn't everything. Neither I nor my staff can be perfect at everything every single day. There's no need to bag on anyone over one bad night. We just need to keep trying to learn and get better for the next time. We're in this for the long haul, after all (see Chapter 7).

EMBRACE YOUR SPONGE-NESS

After years of hard work, we had turned the Grizzlies' fortune around. To celebrate, owners Ken and Bette, surprised Emily and me with a trip to Puerto Vallarta.

For both Emily and me, it was one of our first times out of the country. Not only did it open our eyes to travel, it also opened our eyes to new promotions!

At one point while we were lounging around in Puerto Vallarta, one of the staff came up and offered us a couple of cooling towels to put on our necks. They were just wet, ice-cold towels, nothing more. But, man, were they unbelievably satisfying in the heat.

And it gave me an idea. Leaping up, I grabbed my phone

and emailed the owner of a local heating and cooling company back in town. "I've got a new idea for a promotion at our ballpark," I said. "I want us to create cooling towels and have cooling girls pass them out in the stadium."

"That sounds awesome," the owner said, and we put the idea into play that same year.

If I had never gone to Puerto Vallarta and soaked up the world around me, I never would have had the idea.

That's what being a sponge is all about. It's not going to happen behind a closed door in your office as you sit around doing your own thing. It's going to happen by walking around, talking to people—friends, family, coworkers, and customers—and learning from them. That's how you take it to the next level.

The best sponges can soak up the goods in any environment. Each day, week, month, and year, commit to putting yourself in a new environment, around new people with different ways of doing things, and see where that takes you.

The *how* is up to you. It could be lounging by a pool in Puerto Vallarta. It could be watching documentaries, dropping by a local meet-and-greet event, or going to a local civic meeting. It could be waiting in line at the grocery store. Whatever the case, it's your job to soak it all up. And on that note...

SOAK, SOAK, SOAK

When I was a kid, I didn't read a lot of books. In fact, I would literally cry when I had to do a book report. Actually, thinking about it now, it's a small miracle only the occasional A-minus snuck onto my report card.

I may have stopped with the crying at some point, but this mindset dogged me all the way through college. By the time I got to Gastonia, however, I finally learned the value of stepping back and taking a moment to read and learn new things.

I had to if we were ever going to find any success.

The spongification process started with the greats—Walt Disney, P. T. Barnum, and Bill Veeck. My admiration for Bill Veeck in particular eventually led me to his son Mike's baseball conference (remember that great advice he gave me in Chapter 2?).

However, it was another speaker, an author named Al Fahden, who really drove home the value of living the sponge life.

TWO-DOLLAR BILLS?

There I was, twenty-three years old, unbelievably impressionable, and desperate to make sense of my new job. Suddenly, Fahden burst into the room and started throwing around a bunch of two-dollar bills.

Fahden himself seemed to be just as curious about what was going on as I was. "Why do I have two-dollar bills?" he exclaimed, all the while throwing more handfuls into the air.

After a pause, someone in the crowd offered, "Because they're different?" Fahden began showering him with more bills.

"Not just different. They're memorable!" Fahden beamed.

This guy is crazy, I thought. *I love him.*

A few hundred dollars' worth of two-dollar bills later, Fahden finally began his presentation, opening with a story about his book, *Innovation on Demand*.

"So, I wrote this book," he said. "I decided I had to stay true to the book, so I was going to sell it at a bookstore. However, I wasn't going to just sell it at *any* bookstore. Instead, I bought an entire retail space in Minneapolis, where I'm from, and I started a bookstore. But I only sold one book: my own."

Fahden stocked every corner of the store with his book, setting it up in different sections—self-help, business, leadership—just like you would see at a traditional bookstore. He even had a sign that said, "Shoplifting is encouraged."

It wasn't about the sales. It was about drumming up awareness and getting the book in people's hands. And it worked. His promotion was covered in national publications like *People* and *USA Today*.

SCREW NORMAL!

Thanks to Fahden, I learned one of my greatest life lessons: if it's normal, do the exact opposite.

Later that day, when Mike Veeck told me to get a little crazy with my team, I knew the only way to turn the Grizzlies around was by doing something dramatically different.

In just a day, Fahden and Veeck had transformed my idea of business.

From there, I redoubled my efforts to soak up everything I could. I wanted to learn from the people who had been around the block a few times. I wanted to know what they knew. If grabbing a few pearls of wisdom meant avoiding certain pitfalls, I was all for it.

KNOWLEDGE IS EVERYWHERE

These days, I learn from just about everything—conferences, books, podcasts, you name it. In the process, I've learned that part of living the sponge life is modeling it. That's why at Fans First, we've made sponginess a part of our business culture with our book club.

As I like to tell them, "Read. Your life depends on it."

VEECKING IT UP

By now, you've seen what a big impact Mike Veeck had on my young career. Mike helped drive home the idea that fun, entertainment, and performance are essential to *all* businesses, not just show business.

As the saying goes (and holds true), like father, like son. Just as I was a sponge for Mike's message, Mike was a sponge for the message of his father, the legendary Bill Veeck.

A SPONGE OF A MAN

Bill Veeck owned a lot of baseball teams throughout his career, including the St. Louis Browns and the Chicago White Sox. A brilliant entertainer, he began his journey at twenty-seven years old when he took over a small team in Milwaukee.

Famously, Veeck read everything he could get his hands on, including the encyclopedia. He was known to read five or six books at once—and was said to have died with numerous books (each with its own bookmark) stacked beside him on his deathbed. The books didn't have to be about sports, either. If the subject caught Veeck's attention, he wanted to know more about it.

TAKE THAT LEARNING TO THE STREETS

That's spongeworthy enough, but Bill didn't stop there. He used to go out to bars or saloons and stay until four in the morning. Usually he'd be by himself, with no agenda other than to talk to people, the community, and fans. He loved to pick their brains and get a feel for what they were into and who they were. If the mood struck, they'd even get a little crazy with it.

Outside of the bars, he was a prolific public speaker. Veeck would give free talks anywhere that would have him (see

Chapter 11 for more of this story). One, he knew it was a great way to promote himself and his teams. And two, he saw it as another way to learn and soak up the world around him.

WRINGING IT OUT

Veeck would then take this soaked-up sponge of knowledge and wring it out in the ballpark. Anything was fair game if it got a rise out of the community. Once, he gave away twelve live lobsters and six live squids. Another time, he gave away five hundred pounds of iguana meat.

No one ever knew what Bill Veeck was going to do next, and that's how he liked it.

GO VEECKING

Just as game recognizes game, sponge recognizes sponge.

At Fans First, we've turned Veeck into a verb. Whenever I want to get out, talk to fans, and soak up the wisdom of my community, I tell everyone I'm going *Veecking*. Then, I post up in a restaurant or a bar, turn off my phone, and make myself available to anyone who wants to talk. It never gets old, and I never walk away without a new idea.

We may not be born to conform, but most of us are taught from a young age to be like everyone else. Developing a different mindset takes work. Luckily, it gets easier the more you do it.

So be a sponge. Go Veecking. Leave yourself open to every learning opportunity, whether that opportunity is a book, a new environment, or a conversation with your community. Reach out to your peers, colleagues, and other people in your community. Above all, ask more questions—especially if you're worried that people might think you're dumb. That's the only way to grow.

Do this long enough, and you'll learn to embrace the weird, the crazy, and the new. Curiosity will become your new default, and you'll rise to greet every day with a heart racing with excitement.

That's the mindset that frees you to go bananas. Crazy enough, that's also the mindset we'll be talking about in Chapter 4.

THE YELLOW TUXOMETER

For each question, answer with one of the following: all the time (ten points), sometimes (five points), or never (one point).

1. Have you made dramatically more income over the past two or three years? (Ten points for yes, one point for no.)

2. How often do you read nonfiction/business books?

3. Do you ask your work colleagues/peers questions every day?

4. How often do you go to work conferences?

THE YELLOW TUX BOOKSHELF

Who lives in a pineapple under the sea? SpongeBob SquarePants! I'm not sure whether SpongeBob is much of a reader, but you can learn all about being super absorbent with these books:

- *Great Leaders Grow,* by Ken Blanchard

- *Be Obsessed or Be Average,* by Grant Cardone

- *Think like Zuck,* by Ekaterina Walter

- *Learning Leader* (podcast), by Ryan Hawk

Part II

YELLOW TUXING
YOUR BUSINESS

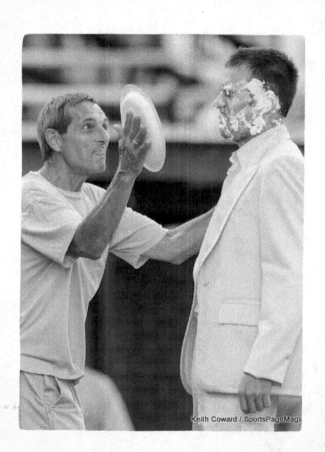

CHAPTER *Four*

A DIFFERENT MINDSET

Innovators are the ones whose dreams are clearer than the reality that tells them they're crazy.

—SIMON SINEK

Nine Line Apparel isn't your normal brand.

They break the rules. They aren't politically correct. They're relentlessly patriotic and are unafraid to tell the world what they stand for. With T-shirts like "Stomp my flag, and I'll stomp your ass" and "Share a round with Isis," they know they're not for everybody—and they're okay with that.[10]

In all these ways, Nine Line stands apart from their com-

10 Learn more about Nine Lines here: https://www.ninelineapparel.com/about-us/

petitors. But the real difference-maker, the thing that makes them a category of one, is their production model.

Founded by brothers Daniel and Tyler Merritt while they were serving in the Army, Nine Line wanted a brand that could move quickly and effectively. "Our company is like a speedboat," Danny says. "We can maneuver very quickly. I can watch the news tonight, find a topic that I believe in, something I want to have a say in, and I can have one of the designers create an idea. Then, we can put it to market on every social media platform in twenty-four hours."

From there, Nine Line lets their fans determine the rest. First, customers pick and design the shirts. Then, a pre-order determines how many are made. If customers don't sign up, they miss out—though another design is always right around the corner.

The model is brilliant. More importantly, it's free and effective. Besides, who better to determine what you're selling than your audience?

Clearly their audience agrees. What began as a home business with just three employees has become the third-fastest-growing retailer in 2016, with over 1.7 million followers on Facebook.[11]

---

11   Seriously, their success is out of this world. Just ask *Inc.* magazine: https://www.inc.com/profile/nine-line-apparel

So why such great success? Maybe it's because they have the audacity to stand for what they believe in. Maybe it's because they take such good care of their fans with free custom decals and koozies with every order.

Or maybe, just maybe, it's because they're willing to get a little crazy.

DIFFERENT MAKES NORMAL NEW

Let's talk about the word "crazy." From now till forever, as author Linda Rottenberg likes to say, crazy is a compliment.[12] It means you're thinking outside the box. It means you and your ideas are on a different level from everyone else. It means you aren't playing things safe.

On "Backwards Night," we followed this mindset to the letter. Fans walked into the stadium backward as we thanked them for coming and asked if they enjoyed the show. The game began in the bottom of the ninth. We had the seventh-inning stretch in what should have been the third inning. We ran all the promotions backwards. And we finished (or, you know, began) the game with the Star Spangled Banner, followed by thirty minutes of pregame announcements.

---

12   See her book, *Crazy Is a Compliment*, in the Yellow Tux Bookshelf at the enc of this chapter.

When you approach things with a different mindset, even the normal things take on a different meaning. I'll tell you, that ovation for the National Anthem was the loudest I'd ever heard—all because it came on the tail end of a dramatic win!

Whenever I hear someone say, "It's always been done that way," I say, "No! Rethink yourself." Tradition and routine don't make something right or even good. And eventually it's going to be flat-out wrong. If you know you can do it better, then *do it better*.

That's what this chapter is all about: going against the grain of what's considered normal. Normal gets normal results. Sure, it's comfortable. But it's also super, super boring.

BE DIFFERENT, NOT RANDOM

Bill Veeck's father was the president of the Chicago Cubs. As a result, Veeck grew up among the titans of baseball, learning a lot about both the game and the business of the game in the process.

One idea burned into his head was that, as America's pastime, baseball was a game of tradition. The game's leaders had a rigid idea of how baseball *should* be, and they made sure others conformed.

The thing was, the more Veeck learned, the more he realized this mindset was doing nothing to grow the sport. Further, the more people he talked to, the more he realized the tradition of baseball wasn't as uniform or sacred as others liked to claim.

When it came time to run his own team, Veeck decided to do something different. He wasn't being different for the sake of being different. His choices weren't scattershot or random. They came from years of observation, reading, learning, and talking to people about the sport, what it could be, and what drew fans to the ballpark.

Both for Veeck and for Fans First Entertainment, it all came down to one question: what business are you *really* in?

For Veeck and me, it was clear, we both realized we were in the entertainment business.

PROFESSIONAL IS BORING

Does the word "professional" excite you? Have you ever pointed out a movie theater or a restaurant to a friend because they were professional?

No one recommends a business because they're professional. They recommend businesses because they're *interesting*—because they're fun, crazy, weird, unique, or bizarre. Good businesses give customers talking points by doing things different and making them *feel good*.

Professional is boring. If you play it safe, you're dead.

EVERY BUSINESS IS IN THE ENTERTAINMENT BUSINESS

We have a responsibility to entertain our customers. If you're all about selling and nothing more, you're going to lose out eventually.

I'm not saying your business needs to throw in song and dance numbers, balloon animals, and confetti. We do, but I get it if that specific flavor of crazy isn't your style, I get it.

That doesn't mean you can't make it fun and memorable. Think about your company and how people buy from you. Think about how you can liven up your process so when your customers walk out, they're telling their friends, "Hey, I bought a copier from so-and-so company. It was so much fun. This is what happened..."

The way I see it, you have two choices: Be stagnant, keep doing your thing, and eventually fade away. Or, accept that "fun" and "professional" aren't mutually exclusive terms. They're complimentary.

Personally, I'd rather go to an accountant that gets a little weird. That way, I know they're relatable, authentic, and probably more committed to doing a good job.

THE PROOF IS ALL AROUND YOU

You already know a little bit about what we do at Fans First Entertainment to, you know, keep the fans first and entertained. We have to be on our game all day, every day. From when the first fan calls at 8:00 a.m. to when our fans leave around 10:30 p.m., every effort and every interaction is designed to get someone to say, "Hey, that was fun," as they walk out the gates.

And that's just at the ballpark. In truth, we have to entertain year-round to keep people interested and coming back. Our fans aren't buying baseball. They're buying fun. That means we have to look at what we're doing with merchandise, with promotions around town, or with digital engagement, like movies and photos.

NIKE KNOWS

Why do people *really* buy from you? It's always more than the product.

Nike sponsors an active lifestyle. Their marketing and promotion isn't about shoes. It's about the lifestyle and experience their shoes help provide. It's about making their customers feel fit, strong, proud, and accomplished.

Nike keeps their mission simple with (see Chapter 5) *Just Do It*. Not only do they represent an active lifestyle. But they represent the best version of yourself. The person who can accomplish anything by just doing it.

THE BLUE OCEAN

Another prime example is Cirque du Soleil. Everybody knows what a circus is. The thing is, the traditional idea of the circus doesn't exactly get people excited anymore. The circus as we know it just shut down after 146 years.

Cirque du Soleil changed that. They took what everybody thought they knew and elevated it to something other-worldly. To achieve this, they took a different mindset, one that authors W. Chan Kim and Renee Mauborgne dubbed the "Blue Ocean Strategy" in their 2005 book of the same name.

Here's the gist of it: businesses usually compete in a brutal, cutthroat environment. Everyone is fighting to undercut the competition, to put out products that are newer, better, and fancier, but ultimately very similar to their competition. It's a bloody mess, or as Kim and Mauborgne might say, a red ocean.

The blue ocean strategy says, "Forget competing on everyone else's terms. Do something different." When you're different, the ocean is calm, blue, and tranquil. No one else is doing what you do, so no one else is competing with you in your ocean.

Does the blue ocean strategy work? You tell me. Other than Cirque du Soleil, how many other modern circuses can you name?

WEIRD WINS

Context is everything. By encouraging yourself to think differently, to take on a new kind of mindset, you will start to uncover what business you are *really* in.

I did this with my business. I knew we weren't just a baseball company. We were an entertainment company, and our product was fun. I did things that went against the status quo—like grandma beauty pageants (more on those in a little bit)—to actively involve my audience in something new and exciting.

There was and always is a method to my madness, but it was still madness.

THE IDEA BOX

Hanging above my office door at Grayson Stadium is a sign with the phrase, "There's something there." Without my realizing it, the phrase had become one of my unofficial mantras. After the 2016 Season drew to a close, Liz, our Marketing Coordinator surprised me by having a sign made out of it.

Admittedly, it's not the most eloquent slogan. Two of the three words are "there," but it works. It's catchy and repeatable, and it has come to embody our entire approach.

I love ideas. I love it when people give me ideas—even if I don't use a good 90 percent of them. I love being in an environment where people want to engage me, where I can walk around the ballpark and hear staff members saying to each other, "There's something there."

That's why I keep every idea in an idea box. I got the approach from the great Bill Veeck, who taught his son,

Mike, that if his house is burning down, the one thing he must grab is the idea box.

Step 1: Fill Your Idea Box

Every off-season at Fans First, we pull out the idea box and have Ideapalooza. All the crazy ideas in our box help get us started, and then when we really get going, we expand to Post-It notes and whiteboards to keep track of everything.

Every idea lives or dies on the chopping block. For each one, we ask ourselves how it could be done—and whether it should be.

Step 2: Question Everything

When an idea makes it onto the chopping block, I ask myself, "Is it different? Is someone else doing that, and if so, how do we make it better or different?" It's crucial to challenge every idea until you can create a different mindset for yourself and your staff.

Step 3: Give Every Idea a Chance

During these Ideapaloozas, Jared, our president, always says, "Whatever it is, there's no negativity allowed." It's a good reminder to all of us, but probably especially me, to be patient.

Even if an idea isn't great, even if I'm sitting in the back wishing we weren't wasting time on an idea, Jared reminds all of us that this is a learning experience. As soon as there's negativity, then people won't open up or put their ideas forward, and that's when the great ideas get buried.

Besides, terrible ideas deserve more credit. I always say that I want either the most creative idea or the worst possible idea. If something is really, truly bad, there's probably something there.

I live for those moments. The second I hear someone say, "That is the worst idea I've ever heard!" my ears perk up.

"Let's stay on this a little bit," I'll say. "*Why* is this so bad? What can we do to make it even worse?"

THE FRUITS OF OUR LABOR

Remember how we talked last chapter about being a sponge? Well, listening and learning from others doesn't mean you have to repeat what they do. Bill Veeck may have learned how to run a baseball club from his dad and other bigwigs, but he made sure not to replicate their success. He carved his own path.

That's what being a sponge is all about. You absorb everything you can, and when the time comes to wring all those ideas out, you make something new. To show you what I mean, let's take a look at a few examples from my own ball clubs.

DIPPIN' AND DANCIN'

No ballpark experience is complete without the vendors. Our vendors, however, are a little different. They don't just sell you ice cream. They sing to you. Want a little Bieber with your Dippin' Dots? Come on down to Grayson Stadium, and they'll make a Belieber out of you.

The thing is, having singing vendors alone is different, but from the Fans First perspective, it's not different enough. We wanted to make sure we had the best singers. Our vendors are trained professionals, not awkward kids testing out their pipes during a summer internship (although that might be funny too).

The thing about good ideas is they often lead to more good ideas. This year in Savannah, we took the singing vendors idea and leveled up. Now we have a break-dancing first base coach who, when he's not showing everyone his moves along the first base line, he represents one of the top dance teams in the country. The night of his debut, he even made #8 on *SportsCenter*'s top ten plays of the day.

EVERYONE LOVES GRANDMAS

I'm going to let you in on a little secret. Sometimes when we put a promotion on the calendar, we have no idea how we're going to execute it—or even if anyone's going to care. It's a risk, but sometimes you just have to stop thinking, start doing, and try out new things.

Such was the case with the Grandma Beauty Pageant. When the week of the pageant finally rolled around, we realized we had no contestants with two days to go until showtime.

"Well," I said, "we promoted this. It's on our schedule. It's on our website. We're having a grandma beauty pageant one way or another, even if we have zero grandmas."

It was time to put things in motion. So, I asked myself: where are the grandmas? Next thing I knew, I was on the phone with a local nursing home. "Hey, we're having a grandma beauty pageant, and we'd love to celebrate some of your grandmas."

"Oh, we would love to do that!" they said.

"Great!" I said. "If you could just provide five grandmas—that would be outstanding."

On pageant day, the gates opened at six o'clock. At 6:15 p.m., there were no grandmas. At 6:30 p.m., still no grandmas. Finally, at about 6:45 p.m., this nursing home van pulled up outside the gate, and out shuffled the grandmas.

It took them at least fifteen minutes to get them to their seats, and probably another fifteen for me to explain my plan to them. They were nodding along and pleasant as could be, but I realized we were probably looking at our slowest promotional night ever—possibly even slower than toddlers vs. turtles night.

None of that mattered once our grandmas hit the field, each escorted by a different player. I introduced each of them with a brief bio, gave them all a chance to do a little dance, and then proceeded to the interviews.

When I asked one woman what magazine she'd most like to appear on the cover of, she didn't miss a beat. Grabbing the mic, she said, "*Playboy*, of course!"

The crowd lost their minds, propelling her to granny greatness. After she was announced the Grizzlies Grandma of the Year, we came out with a sash and a big bouquet, and the crowd once again gave her a standing ovation.

Looking back, the thing that sticks with me most was the look on her face and the way she teared up and smiled when she was announced the winner. What began as a goofy promotion ended up being such a wonderful, moving moment for her and her family. I'll never forget that.

Moments like that don't just happen out of thin air. When you commit to doing things a little different, you never know when the magic might happen.

WHO FARTED?

On the other hand, sometimes the magic eludes you. For instance, I thought Flatulence Fun Night and Salute to Underwear Night were guaranteed crowd pleasers as long as we took the ideas and ran with them.

That meant going all-in (more on that in Chapter 8). Generic T-shirts, bats, or baseballs wouldn't cut the cheese on Flatulence Fun Night. We gave away whoopee cushions and held a bean burrito eating contest and a farting contest on the field. Unfortunately, the whoopee cushions

I ordered came back half the size they should have been, and the crowd never really got into the on-field promotions.

Same thing for Salute to Underwear Night. I would have thought more people wanted a free pair of tighty whities with our logo on the backside. I even told people to wear their own underwear over their pants to get free admission. What a great promotion, right? Well, the media showed up but after only about three or four hundred people showed up, the answer was clearly no.

Do I regret these promotional misfires? Nope. We didn't lose much by taking the risk, the people who did show up had fun, and we learned a lot about what we could get away with next time if we decided to get really crazy.

BRINGING THE OUTSIDE IN

When you do things different, you do them better. As we already talked about in Chapter 2, that means bringing in the best people to help you out.

A lot of the time, this means bringing in people who don't even know the first thing about baseball. This happens a lot when we bring in performers.

Often, however, their unfamiliarity with the sport proves

to be an asset. Take the story of Miles, one of our on-field personalities who we first brought in as a theater and improv expert from Lexington, Kentucky. He had never been to a ball game before he met us.

During his first week on the job, he looked over at our bat boy (the person responsible for collecting the batters' bats) and said, "Hey, what if we have that kid dress up as Batman?"

We bought the suits, found a kid willing to do it, debuted Batboy that week, and shot a great video of the whole thing.

The Batboy pun seems obvious in retrospect (seriously, how has no other team ever done this?), but it took a baseball outsider to come up with it.

NO RÉSUMÉS

Another way Fans First stands out is that we don't look at resumes. I've never seen any of my staff's resumes, and they know it.[13]

Our philosophy comes down to this: We don't care what our future staff did in the past. We only care that they're

---

13 Want the inside look on how we hire? Check out our search for the next Bananas coach on YouTube (keywords: "Savannah's Next Great Bananas Coach").

fun, they fit into our culture, and they're excited to learn and contribute.

Resumes don't tell you that—but you can figure it out pretty quickly by striking up a conversation with them or watching how they interact with others.

If we looked at resumes, we probably wouldn't be successful hiring outsiders like Will, the Bananas' Director of Entertainment for the first two seasons. Just like Miles, Will came from a theater and improv background. And also like Miles, Will knew essentially nothing about sports other than what he picked up watching some Kentucky basketball.

For example, during his first game with us, Will turned to the promotions team and asked, "Does the home team always bat second, in the bottom of the inning?" We confirmed this, explaining that's how it works in baseball.

It's funny, but none of it matters. Will doesn't need to know the nuances of baseball to be a great director of entertainment. He's the genius behind ideas like "Sing in the Blank," "Banana in the Pants," and "The Shower Squad"[14]—ideas that never would have come from someone with a baseball background.

---

14 Apparently, we like having grown men play dress-up—or in this case dress down. Between innings, the Shower Squad comes out wearing nothing but towels. They're supposed to deliver water to the umpires, but instead, they proceed to pour water all over themselves and clean off with loofahs.

The more you surround yourself with outsiders who are good at what they do, and the more you trust in what someone wants to be rather than what they've been, the more that person will bring to your organization. That's how you stand out not only on difference, but also on quality.

NEW WINS

Sometimes, to bring the outside in, you actually have to get up and go travel outside. To think different, you've got to get out of your comfort zone.

Just look at Howard Shultz, the man who caffeinated Seattle—and then the world. Back in the seventies, he was comfortable in his Seattle ways, living his Seattle life. But eventually, he got restless. He craved something new.

MAKE WAY FOR ITALY

Shultz had always wanted to travel, so he set a course for Italy. He packed his bags, hopped on a plane, and immersed himself in their culture.

More than anything, he couldn't believe the quality of their coffeehouses. They weren't just places to grab a cup o' joe and go. They were all about community.

Soon, the light bulb in his mind flickered on, and Starbucks was born.

CRAZY LIKE A FOX

Some people thought he was crazy. What gave Shultz the right to change things? Why would anybody want to pay out the nose just for coffee? What was wrong with a fifty-cent cup from the local diner?

As it turns out, those vocal critics were the minority. Consumers were very curious for a new coffee experience. And through it, they discovered what Shultz was really selling: community. If shelling out a few extra bucks allowed them to socialize in a comfortable, welcoming environment, it was worth it.

Starbucks and modern coffeehouse culture probably wouldn't have happened if Shultz hadn't gone to Italy. He needed to immerse himself in an experience that was fundamentally different from what he was used to back home.

It's very easy to get narrow-sighted with your business. But when you do this, five, ten, or twenty years can pass by with you hardly looking up and taking in the world around you. And when you finally do, you realize that you were just riding the hamster wheel the whole time. You didn't actually take your business anywhere.

THERE'S A WHOLE WORLD OUT THERE

It's never easy to push yourself outside of your comfort zone. But when you do, you remember there's this whole world out there full of great ideas to learn, internalize, and make something new.

Once Shultz found that spark of an idea, he was determined to make it work. And so, like Walt Disney and so many other business leaders like him, Shultz went all-in.

Anyone can think up something different, but that's only the first step. Once you've come up with your great idea, you have to sell it. And that means simplifying it into a core concept that people understand.

In Chapter 5, we will discuss how to take your big ideas and turn them into something tangible. Get ready! This is going to take every creative gear you have. There's nothing easy about getting simple and making your ideas real.

THE YELLOW TUXOMETER

For each question, answer with one of the following: all the time (ten points), sometimes (five points), or never (one point).

1. Do you keep notes somewhere with ideas and lessons?

2. Do you drive the same way to work every day?

3. How often does your Monday–Friday morning routine change?

4. Do you take cold showers?

THE YELLOW TUX BOOKSHELF

Without a plan, you're just being different for the sake of it. You'll probably have some fun that way, but you might not see the business results you were hoping for. Here are some books to help you embrace what makes you different and turn it into a winning business formula.

- *Blue Ocean Strategy*, by Chan Kim

- *Fascinate*, by Sally Hogshead

- *Play Bigger*, by Christopher Lochhead, Al Ramadan, Dave Peterson, and Kevin Maney

- *Linchpin and Purple Cow*, by Seth Godin

- *Friction*, by Jeff Rosenblum

- *Rebel Rules,* by Chip Conley

- *Reinventors*, by Jason Jennings

- *Crazy Is a Compliment*, by Linda Rottenberg

CHAPTER *Five*

SIMPLIFY, SIMPLIFY, SIMPLIFY

If you can make things simple, you can move mountains.

—STEVE JOBS

Apple products are known for keeping it simple—and for causing a frenzy. When they first put out the iPod, they did the exact opposite of every other mp3 player on the market. They *eliminated* as many buttons and features as they could, simplifying the browsing experience to a scroll wheel and a central button.

By the time the iPod rolled out, the product's mastermind, Apple cofounder Steve Jobs, already had a decades-long track record of pursuing simplicity. When Jobs went to Pixar, for example, the company was failing.

After investing $50 million of his own money to keep things afloat, Jobs brought in Lawrence Levy as Pixar's CFO. Levy took one look at the company and realized they had four departments—four areas of focus—and none of them was making real money.

At the same time, both Levy and Jobs realized that Pixar had some of the most creative minds in the industry. Together, they decided the only way to move forward was to cut out every part of the business that wasn't successful and put all their energy into a new venture—a feature-length film called *Toy Story*.

Today, Pixar and *Toy Story* are household names, and it almost feels like their success was predestined. But it wasn't. If Jobs and Levy hadn't pushed the company to simplify (and to go all-in, which we'll talk about in Chapter 8), if Pixar themselves hadn't put all their energy into storytelling, none of that would have happened.

Jobs brought this lesson back with him to Apple a few years later. From the late nineties to today, everything at Apple is about simplicity. Their slogan is a sparse (but powerful) two words: *Think different*. Their products, packaging, and storefronts all feel expansive and clutter-free.

Even after Steve Jobs' passing, Apple's commitment to

simplicity remains incredibly consistent—and a huge part of their success.

SIMPLE IS MEMORABLE

A grand idea doesn't have to be complicated. Sometimes, being different is being simple. In this chapter, we will discuss the importance of boiling down your ideas to their elemental form and asking yourself, "In one word, what do I want to be known for?" By the end of this chapter, you'll be able to describe what you do in five seconds, including your mission and your marketing strategy.

EASY TO REMEMBER, EASY TO SHARE

Today's most successful companies all have one thing in common: they make thing easy.

There's a reason for this. The simpler the message, the easier it is to remember, and the easier it is to share. In other words, if a five-year-old can remember your message, then you've got a good message.

WHAT DO YOU WANT TO BE KNOWN FOR?

To simplify your message, you must have a deep, elemental understanding of what you want to be known for.

You can see this in all the best companies. For instance, when you think Google, you think "search." Actually, you might just think "google," since the company has become so deeply associated with web searches that it's become synonymous with it—something I'm sure Yahoo still isn't happy about.

How does Google do it? Look at their website. With a scant nine or so words, a logo, and a search field, Google makes it clear what you're supposed to do.

REMEMBER WHAT YOU'RE BEST AT?

To determine what you want to be known for, think back to Chapter 2. Whatever you're best at, that's what you should be known for.

Don't worry, you can do other things too. Google doesn't *only* offer internet searches. They also have incredibly popular email and video services in Gmail and YouTube. But you can't be best at everything—and you muddy your message if you try to claim otherwise.

BE THE *YOU* OF YOUR INDUSTRY

You know how the brand name Kleenex has come to represent all tissues? You know how "Google it" is the catch-all suggestion for researching something on the internet? Their names have become synonymous with what they do.

It's even better when people use *you* to describe what *they* do. I've heard plenty of companies describe themselves this way. Maybe they're the Uber of food delivery services. Maybe they're the Netflix of educational videos. Maybe they're the Savannah Bananas of synchronized swimming.[15]

Here's an example I like to use. Dabo Swinney was hired as head coach of the Clemson University football team in 2008. During an early morning meeting, one member of the board of trustees said, "We want to create a football program that's like some of the other great programs in the country," and then he proceeded to name some of his favorite programs.

Swinney listened to all this and replied, "Sir, I appreciate your vision, but mine is much bigger than that. My vision is to create a program where they want to be like us."[16]

---

15 For the record, I have no idea what being the Savannah Bananas of synchronized swimming would entail, although we have had grown men splash around in kiddie pools as part of one of our promotions.

16 Jon Gordon. "Championship Lessons." *The Jon Gordon Companies.* (January 16, 2017). http://www.jongordon.com/positivetip/championship-lessons.html

That's the dream, right there. If people want to be the *you* of their industry, you know you've left an impact.

YOU CONFUSE, YOU LOSE

Why simplify? As Donald Miller of StoryBrand says, "You confuse, you lose."

This philosophy drives Miller's work with companies. Usually, his first stop is their website. To Miller, a good website can grab and hold the customer's attention within five seconds.

That's not a lot of time. But then again, it's the internet. That's all the time you're going to get before your visitor moves on to something more interesting.

Miller's approach works great for the web, but in reality it can be applied anywhere. Just think of Geico's old slogan, "It's so easy, a caveman could do it." That's about as literal as it gets, but it's what every company should aspire to.

WHAT TO DO WITH YOUR FIVE SECONDS?

Friction author Jeff Rosenblum says, "Whoever says the most in the least amount of words, wins." Now that you know your message, it's time to refine it. Your goal is to describe what you do in five seconds.

To keep your message simple, I have a simple process:

1. Write down your message as a thirty-second elevator pitch.
2. Cut out all the fluff until you're down to a single sentence.

Don't bang your head against the wall if you can't pull this off overnight. Refining your message takes work. As you'll see a little bit later in the chapter, it's taken us ten years to refine our message at Fans First Entertainment—and we're still working on the next step I'm about to share.

THE ONE-WORD MINDSET

When you think Google, you think "search." As people, we're always looking for ways to remember the smallest amount of information. It's your job to facilitate that.

What single word do you want people to associate with you?

This is the holy grail of simplicity. If you can do it, I tip my big, yellow, top hat to you.

Why? Well, full transparency, we're still working on it ourselves.

We've got the five-second pitch: "Fans first. Entertain always." Breaking it down farther than that is a challenge. But it's the exercise that makes it worth it.

What do you stand for? What do you want to be known for? This is a great starting point.

WHAT DO YOU ACTUALLY DO?

Most companies don't know their own mission statement. They might have an idea, but usually the actual phrasing eludes them. It's too long. It's filled with lofty marketing jargon. It's uninspiring.

It's also not presented well. Most mission statements are buried in a thirty-page handbook. New hires might come across it once during training, but otherwise it's lost in a drawer somewhere.

No one reads it. No one cares. Nothing happens.

THE FANS FIRST IDEA REFINERY

It took ten years for my company and I to simplify our

brand's message, mission, and purpose. We had several different iterations of our core values—bringing people together, taking care of others, having fun within a community—but it always came back to two words: "fans first."

We knew this nailed the first part of our message, but something was missing. What about our show? What about the circus? How could we describe this part of our mission?

Finally, someone said, "Well, we entertain."

That got us closer. "Yeah," someone else said, "if we're putting our fans first, if we're doing it all the time, how often are we entertaining them?"

"Well, we *always* entertain," came the reply.

And they were right. We sing into the phone and play ridiculous hold music. We dance with fans as they come through the front gate. We sing Bieber songs at our concessions.

Even in the offseason, we're always up to something. Split (our mascot) and I regularly attend local events, ceremonies, and celebrations. We've also had a ton of fun with videos, like the one where our pep band plays Europe's

"The Final Countdown" as a staff member microwaves lunch,[17] or the one where Split dances with Jared, our team president, to the song from *Beauty and the Beast*.[18]

Yep, we're always having fun. We're always entertaining. Making that the second part of our mission seemed like a no-brainer.

Our motto, "Fans first, entertain always," works because it's simple. Everyone can understand it, meaning everyone knows what to expect. These four words make everything else we do possible.

EVERYONE IS A FAN

When the first part of your motto is "fans first," your job is to create fans out of everybody. A lot of companies don't approach it this way. They define their typical customer by region or demographic.

By our reckoning, everyone is a fan or has the potential to be one. And this approach is paying off. We get fans we never imagined—people in their seventies and eighties,

---

17 Yep, the Banana Band had trouble adjusting to the office in the 2017 off-season (YouTube keywords: "Savannah This Is Bananas: Banana Band")

18 It's a tale as old as time (YouTube keywords: "Savannah Banana and the Beast").

people from other corners of the globe, and even people who swore off baseball a long time ago.

That's what happens when you don't overthink things and pigeonhole yourself. People know we entertain always, and they turn out expecting a show. Most people think of baseball and other sports as a male-dominated field. However, the majority of our fans are women.

Keeping things simple doesn't limit you. It creates possibilities. The simpler your message, the more it resonates with people.

WHO ARE YOUR BIGGEST FANS?

"Fans first, entertain always" are only words. It's our job to live up to that promise, to add credibility and substance to it. We repeat it as often as we can so not only do our fans know what we stand for, but so we remember the standard we hold *ourselves* to.

Every chance I get, I ask my staff, "Who are our biggest fans, guys?"

The senior staff already knows the answer, but they let the newbies look around and think about it.

"Who's here sixteen hours a day?" I continue. "Who's here *eighteen* hours a day? Who's wearing our gear all the time?"

At this point, usually one of them will look up and say, "Us?"

"Yes. You got that right," I say. "You guys are our biggest fans."

This is why we're Fans First Entertainment and not "Customers First Entertainment." Don't get me wrong. Our customers are our fans—and they mean *everything* to us. However, we learned years ago that if we put our people first, they turn around and do the same thing for our customers.

To hold ourselves to this, we follow the Fans First Way: Always Be Caring, Different, Enthusiastic, Fun, Growing, and Hungry. These are our commandments. It helps us ensure that both our staff and our fans always feel like they belong.

As we've grown over the years and added more staff, the value of these ABCDs has grown increasingly apparent. It communicates a big concept in as few words as possible, offering new staff fundamental guidance when they're confronted with a new situation.

SIMPLICITY RULES

Something I hate is the word "policy." If you ask anyone on my staff what our policies are, they will tell you there are none.

Policy kills businesses. "No shoes, no shirt, no this, no that"—every time you tell people "no," you open a can of worms that will wreak havoc on everyone it touches.

Instead, of policies, we just ask ourselves one question: "What's Fans First?"

It's a simple question, but the point of it is that it eliminates decision making. It means that whatever you do, no matter the situation, just remember to put the fans first.

I can walk up to a new staff member mere hours into the job and ask, "Hey, what does 'Fans First' mean to you?"

They say, "To take care of people."

I say, "Yes. Always. No matter what."

This means if a fan drops some food they ordered, we take care of it without making them pay again. It means fans can even bring their own food and drink into the game.

We're here to provide a *worthwhile* experience. We're not here to tell our fans no.

Naturally, there are some limitations. We care about our fans' well-being, so we wouldn't want to create any potentially dangerous situations. But even then, we hold to our mission: Fans First.

FIRST IMPRESSIONS MATTER

We're in the business of first impressions. *Every* business is in the business of first impressions.

Despite this, I'm always amazed at how many offices and restaurants have no one to welcome you when you walk in. All you get is a "Please be seated" sign and maybe a bell, and then you're expected to wait.

The first impression and the last impression are everything. It doesn't matter what you sell; your fans want to feel like they're welcome.

That's where Keke, our Director of First Impressions, comes in.

Keke came to the Bananas as an introverted intern. Her first day with us, she had a lot of trouble opening up, but

I knew she had some magic inside her. I did what I could to reassure her, encouraging her not only to learn as much as she could, but also to have fun.

One night, I needed her to sell beer in the plaza. It was a new challenge for her, and she was visibly nervous. I wanted to break the tension. "Hey, Keke," I said. "You've got nothing to lose tonight. People may remember you, or they may not. All I want you to do is give them a good first impression. Yell for beer. Do what you can to get people to come over to your table and buy from you, but do it in a way that's fun for you. Enjoy yourself!"

By midgame, I walked over to the plaza and found a huge line at her station. There stood Keke, as bright and animated as I'd ever seen, yelling, "Come get tipsy with Keke!" She was singing songs and laughing along with the crowd.

The next day, her energy hadn't let up. Every phone call was met with a booming, "Savannah Bananas! This is Keke!" When people walked into the office, she'd walk over and either shake their hand or give them a big hug. A switch had gone on in her head, and she realized what her life could actually be like if she simply let go and had fun. I knew she had something in her, but I didn't know she'd grow to become one of our best employees.

Since her tipsy days, Keke has taken on an expanded role on our staff, masterfully overseeing 160–200 people during every event—and she's only twenty-three! The work she's put in for us has been nothing short of amazing, and it all started when she embraced the art of first impressions.

LAST IMPRESSIONS MATTER TOO

When our fans leave our ballpark, upwards of twenty staff members are there to wave them off. It might sound excessive, but fans email us all the time to tell us how much they appreciate it.

Here, we wanted to give fans the opposite impression of a restaurant at closing time. I bet you know what I mean. You've probably walked into an empty restaurant a half-hour before closing time.

When you did, I'd wager there was no one there to greet you—that all you saw was a bare-bones staff quietly cleaning and locking up.

I'm not here to knock restaurant staff. We at Fans First understand the long hours people in the service industry work. We understand how exhausting it can be running around on your feet all day. We've been there plenty of times ourselves.

That said, we've learned that even closing time should be a celebration. Sure, we're tired. Everyone from the players to the fans is tired at the end of one of our shows. But what a wonderful thing if we can make one last meaningful impression on our fans as they're walking out of the gates.

The Fans First staff makes it a point to finish our work and be at the gates *before* the final out. That way, we can wave good-bye to as many fans as possible. Not only can we feel the difference we're making for our fans, we can also see firsthand how much fun everyone had.

The longer we stand there smiling at people, the more thank-yous, hugs, and waves we receive. What better way to leave work on a high note? It may sound funny, but shaking hands, giving hugs, and saying good-bye at the end of a good night is still one of the best parts of my job.

EVEN THE RAINOUTS MATTER

If you really want to see what Fans First Entertainment is all about, come to a game that gets rained out. While we realize we can't control the weather (although I've got my top weather scientists hard at work on this very task), we *can* control the experience.

The second the rain rolls in, we go into full Fans First

overdrive. We'll perform little skits and dances with the promotions team. We'll send out the staff and players to do tarp slides. We'll pull out giant inflatable monkeys and have surfing monkey races. We'll send out the Bananas Pep Band to lead the crowd in sing-a-longs. We'll have *Family Feud*-style contests with pies as prizes. We'll bring our dancing first base coach into the grandstands for dance-offs. We do whatever we need to do to keep the show rolling—even if the game is ground to a halt.

From an operations standpoint, nothing makes me prouder than moments like this. During rainouts, our staff lines up at the gates with plenty of umbrellas and offers to walk guests to their cars. One of our interns took this a step further one day when she walked an older gentleman all the way home. When I asked her about it, all she said was, "Fans first."

Efforts like this are part of the larger concept—creating the perfect customer experience. It's another simple idea, but it's one you've got to keep at until you're blue in the face.

In *Customers for Life*, author Carl Sewell explains how he literally hired street cleaners to take care of the areas leading up to his car dealerships. Why? Because he figured a customer was worth hundreds of thousands of dollars if he could make them a customer for life.

When we think of the perfect fan experience, we're not just thinking about how many people there are to greet them when they enter or leave the ballpark. We're thinking about every touchpoint—websites, phone calls, merchandise, you name it. We literally call fans to thank them when they order tickets or merchandise just so they know how much they mean to us. Oh, and we also treat their order like it's a precious treasure, as our confirmation emails indicate:

> *Congrats, you just made the best decision of your day! Just now, as your order came in, our entire staff celebrated with a parade around Grayson Stadium! After numerous songs, dances, high fives and Gatorade showers, we are hoisting your items into the air! There is maximum security, including twenty-four-hour surveillance, and your order will be taken care of right away! Now sit back, relax, and mentally prepare for the best purchase of your life with the Savannah Bananas. Go Bananas!*

Every interaction is a chance to have fun with your fans. Always show them you care—and then show them again the next chance you get.

BELONG EVERYWHERE

Brian Chesky, founder of Airbnb, went through a long

process of his own on his way to simplifying his brand message and getting to what his company *really* did. At first, it was just about housing people. In fact, to begin with, all Airbnb users had to have an airbed, and that was it.

This gradually caused Chesky to realize his business went beyond a place to sleep. That wasn't the business he was actually in.

To Chesky, the question became, "Why do people shell out hundreds for a night in a hotel?" For tons of reasons: They have great beds, hot showers, complimentary breakfasts, and convenient locations. In all, they offer an experience.

Chesky wanted to apply the same aspects to the Airbnb community, but at a more affordable cost and anywhere in the world. His mission was to help his community feel they belonged anywhere. So, that became their slogan: *Belong anywhere.* Ever since this pivot, Airbnb has been expanding like crazy.

Just like with Apple, simplicity isn't only in Airbnb's slogan, but in their interface as well. A big fan of Steve Jobs' three-click philosophy for the iPod, Chesky made sure Airbnb reservations were only three clicks away on their website as well.[19]

---

19   To learn more about Chesky and his Airbnb philosophy, I highly recommend checking out this podcast (Google keywords "Art 19 Bonus Uncut Interview Airbnb's Brian Chesky").

The process of simplicity is gradual and consists of trial and error. You can't expect to nail your mission statement and brand identity in one session. It can take years to find the one or two words that sum up what your company is. In the end, and as we will discuss in Chapter 6, all great things can come from taking small steps.

THE YELLOW TUXOMETER

This time, you've got a whole bunch of yes or no questions. Give yourself ten points for yes, and one point for no.

1. Do you have fewer than fifty articles of clothing?

2. Would your spouse describe you as extremely organized?

3. Do you have a personal mission statement?

4. Can you say what your business does in one sentence?

5. Can you describe your perfect customer?

THE YELLOW TUX BOOKSHELF

Who knew there was so much to keeping things simple? You ask me, it's one of the great ironies of the world. But while we're on the subject, we might as well dig even deeper with these great reads.

- *Pumpkin Plan*, by Mike Michalowicz

- *Simply Brilliant*, by William Taylor

- *Insanely Simple*, by Ken Seagell

- *Think Simple*, by Ken Seagull

- *Simplify*, by Richard Koch

- *Essentialism*, by Greg McKeowen

- *One Thing*, by Jay Papisan

- *One Word*, by Jon Gordon

- *Keep It Simple*, by Joe Calloway

CHAPTER *Six*

SMALL STEPS

The key to realizing a dream is to focus not on success, but significance.

—OPRAH WINFREY

What's the difference between success and significance? Put simply, success is something you earn for yourself. It could be well-intentioned, but there's a selfishness to it.

Significance, on the other hand, isn't about you. Instead, it's about the impact you have on *others*.

Lasting significance is also harder to achieve—even if you're Oprah. Oprah could have settled for the early success she'd found in the eighties, but she decided to become more than a popular talk show host. She wanted to create a lasting impact.

Today, we can see the results of her impact everywhere.

Her *O* magazine lines the checkout aisles of grocery stores. Her book club recommendations turn authors into overnight best-sellers (thanks, Oprah!). The perks and surprise gifts she offers her fans have become legendary.

Oprah didn't build her media empire all at once. That would have been impossible. Instead, everything we know and love about Oprah today is the result of many years of many small steps.

SMALL STEPS, YOU SAY?

In the last chapter, we discussed the process of simplifying what you do, your main message, and your mission statement. In this chapter, we are going to talk about the small steps everyone must take to fulfill a larger mission.

Small steps are born out of simplifying. Once you know what your mission statement is, you have to live it every day.

For us, that means constantly looking at what new promotions we can produce or what new things we can throw at our fans. If it's new and it's different, and if we think it fits our mission statement, we find a way to make it work.

DO SMALL BETS ALWAYS WORK?

Small bets aren't a sure thing. That's okay. They don't have to be.

Remember the Flatulence Fun and Salute to Underwear nights? They're fun to talk about now (hey, I thought they were fun to talk about then too), but they were big ol' duds. We won't do those again.

But because they were small steps, because we didn't bet the farm on them (more on that in Chapter 8), they didn't hurt us. We learned what we could learn and moved on.

IT'S ALL ABOUT THE FLOPPORTUNITIES

Flops are opportunities. Any time you make a mistake, you have a perfect learning moment. You have data. You have a case study.

Look at Taco Bell. They are constantly trying new things. The fast food chain throws new, gimmicky menu items at their customers all the time. They constantly mix different ingredients, which sometimes leads to whacky partnerships with Doritos for a new kind of taco. They're also trying to convince America to eat tacos for breakfast, with crazy items like Waffle Tacos (hey, there's breakfast burritos. Why not breakfast tacos?).

These days, some Taco Bells are even serving alcohol and hosting weddings! You heard that right: $600 will get you a Taco Bell Wedding, complete with a twelve-pack of tacos, a sauce packet bouquet and garter, and "just married" T-shirts.[20]

They've had major wins and total flops. Each success and failure, they took notes and learned when they took a taco too far. With small steps, the wins outweigh the flops.

That's what small steps are all about—experimentation at a low cost.

You must be willing to roll the dice from time to time. It's about refining what you're good at and seeing what opportunities are out there.

IT'S NOT ALL ABOUT MARKETING

It's easy to think small bets are all about marketing, promotions, and public outreach. That's part of it, but remember, small bets are business decisions. That means they apply to *all* aspects of your business—including your staff.

Ben, the videographer for the Bananas began as a summer intern. It wasn't supposed to be a full-time job. We may

20 No, seriously. Just Google "Taco Bell How to Get Married."

play to sellout crowds every night, but we're still a college-level team. A full-time videographer didn't feel like something we could afford. It felt like a big bet.

But then he showed us what he could do. Every day, he'd show up, write scripts, film scenes, and edit movies. Each clip got people talking and sharing on social media. These days, videos like "Can't Stop the Peeling" have received almost 200,000 views.[21]

I was blown away. We all were. From there, hiring him full-time felt not only like a small bet, but a safe one. It took small steps to get there. Once we saw his talent and what he could offer even in a part-time position, we had all the evidence we needed that this was the right decision.

These days, having a full-time videographer feels like a no-brainer. We're an entertainment company. Shouldn't we have at least one person on the staff whose main job is entertainment?

THAT'S THE TICKET

A lot of businesses are afraid to take a risk with a small step. They fear they'll throw something *too* crazy at their fans.

---

21 Can't stop, won't stop—the peeling, that s (YouTube keywords: "Savannah Bananas Can't Stop the Peeling").

Nonsense. Failure is part of the game. Accept that and move on.

Three years ago, we wanted to do something cool with our tickets. Everyone was either selling small, easily portable tickets or digital passes. And, well, since that's what passed for normal, we knew we needed to do the exact opposite.

So, we landed on a grand idea—the world's largest ticket.

Our tickets were life-sized posters about two or three feet long with huge pictures on them. We printed thousands of them. They looked great. We couldn't wait to share them with our fans.

The fans did *not* share our enthusiasm.

We loved the tickets because they were different and unique. The fans hated them because they were really, really inconvenient. All we had done was make their lives more difficult.

The idea may have fallen flat on its face, but it was a small experiment. No harm done. The fans may not have been happy about it, but at least it was a memorable (and forgivable) mistake. The fans were still talking about it a year later.

By that time, we had taken a different approach with our tickets. We still didn't want to do what everyone else did, but we knew we could do better than our giant tickets.

So we went bananas. That is, we hired a company to cut each ticket into the shape of a banana. When a fan presented us with one at the gate, we would rip off the top of the peel and keep the stub to track attendance.

People *loved* it. It was unique without being inconvenient, and it directly correlated with what Fans First is all about—going bananas!

Small steps are small bets. Even if it doesn't pan out—and sometimes it won't—you have to take chances to move forward. Trust your fans, show them you're trying, and they'll be sure to take note.

GETTIN' WARBY WITH IT

Let's talk about Warby Parker. As of this writing, they're only seven years old, but they're already a billion-dollar company. How did they pull this off?

Innovation. Punching fear in the face. Making every small step *count*.

Warby's is known not only for selling fashionable glasses for a good price, but also for providing an excellent customer experience. They were the first online eyewear service of their kind, giving customers a one-click option for stylish frames. And like Tom's Shoes (see Chapter 11), they were mission-based—for every pair of glasses sold, they donate another pair to communities in need.

HOT OUT OF THE GATE

The Warby Parker experiment took off right away, selling thousands of dollars' worth of glasses and generating a twenty-thousand-person waiting list.

In addition to their basic service, they made a small bet with a home try-on program. People enjoyed brick-and-mortar glasses stores because they could try frames on without making a commitment. No online retailer had offered a similar service up to that point. But the way Warby Parker saw it, a home try-on program could eliminate a pain point and further separate them from the competition.

This small bet paid off in a big way. In fact, the program was so popular that customers actually crashed the Warby Parker website.

DOUBLE DOWN

Selling too much was a great problem to have. However, their founder, Neil Blumenthal, worried they were leaving money on the table. So, he took another small bet, opening his apartment to anyone who wanted to come over and try on some glasses.

When even Blumenthal's apartment was overwhelmed, the company opened small pop-up stores to keep up with demand. People went crazy for their service, so Warby Parker made sure to get crazy with them.

THE ROAD SHOW

Eventually, this led to another small bet—converting an old school bus into a traveling pop-up store. They went from city to city with sweatshirts, mugs, and—of course—glasses. Aside from generating goodwill, they also gathered data. Wherever bus stops were most successful, they built a store. From something as simple as selling glasses, they turned a series of small bets into a retail phenomenon.

What a story and what an inspiration. I'm always looking at companies like Warby Parker to see what small bets I can make next. These days, I'm considering all sorts of things.

- What would a Banana Bus be like, what kind of show could we bring around the country, and how could we make it different from Warby Parker's?
- What if our bullpens had actual bulls? What would that cost? Would that be safe? Would our fans get the joke?
- What's a good way to start a joke rivalry with the CPL's newest team, the Macon Bacon? Right now, my inspiration is a Sarah McLachlan—inspired PSA where I implore the people of Macon to save the pigs and go bananas instead.[22]

Sometimes when I'm chasing one of these ideas, I catch myself looking at the craziest stuff on my computer in the office. Do you know how much a miniature bull costs? Did you even know they *had* miniature bulls? I do.

In Chapter 7, we are going to take your small steps and teach you how to make them work out for you in the long game.

I'm all for small bets, but let's not confuse those with short-term, financially motivated decisions. Those are company killers. Don't even give them a second thought.

---

22 This one became a reality—and it was a big hit. Barstool and other news outlets even picked it up (YouTube keywords: "Official Protest Announcement Stop the Macon Bacon").

Every decision you make and every small step you take should go toward serving a larger purpose.

THE YELLOW TUXOMETER

For each question, answer with one of the following: all the time (ten points), sometimes (five points), or never (one point).

1. How often do you try new things? Restaurants? Meals? TV shows?

2. How often do friends or coworkers question your ideas?

3. How many times do your ideas fail or never come to fruition?

4. How often do your friends jokingly tell you that you are crazy?

THE YELLOW TUX BOOKSHELF

In *What About Bob?*, Bill Murray's title character learned precisely how powerful baby steps were in helping him reach his goals. What works for Bob can work for your business, especially when you're armed with this one book, *Little Bets*, by Peter Sims.

CHAPTER *Seven*

THE LONG GAME

I'm not telling you it's going to be easy; I'm telling you it's going to be worth it.

—ARTHUR WILLIAMS

"We messed up," I said to the staff who were gathered around me after the ball game was over and the fans had all left.

It was fireworks night in Gastonia. We wanted the game to be "all you can eat," but we made the short-term decision not to splurge. We only had three grills, resulting in an hour-long wait for food, and most of our fans missed most of the show.

"This is on me," I continued.

More grills would have cost more, but at least our fans would have left *as fans* at the end of the night. We could've invested in double the grills and double the staff and still come out on top.

"If I went to that game today, I might not come back," I said. "That kills me to my core, guys, and it's because we played the short game tonight."

SETTLING IN FOR THE LONG HAUL

Playing the short game usually hurts in the long run. It's better to struggle early for a later payoff than the other way around. The long game will always pay off better than the short game down the road.

THE WINDING ROAD TO SUCCESS

Success is rarely just a day away. It's not waiting for you around the corner. It's a long, long journey.

Along that journey, you're going to get beat up. You're going to put out fires. You're going to face challenges that will make you want to pack it all in and move on with your life.

That's scary.

LET YOUR MISSION STATEMENT GUIDE YOU

The way I see it, there are only two ways to fight your fear and keep moving ahead.

1. Winning on the kinds of small bets we talked about in the last chapter.
2. Setting incremental, long-term goals designed to help you keep your eye on the prize.

Unite these two goals in your mission statement. The second you forget that, you lose sight of the long-term goal and fall victim to the short-term trap.

That's what happened that night in Gastonia. We thought it would be good to cut costs and try to save money for the long season ahead. Sure, it's good to save money when you can—but not if that means ignoring your mission statement.

We failed to live up to both parts of our mission. Fans first? I doubt the people in the back of the hour-long line felt that way. Entertain always? What's so fun about missing the show—doubly so if you want to get back in line for seconds?

The long game is the long game for a reason. Take shortcuts where you can, but beware of the shortcuts that pull you off course.

WHAT EXACTLY *IS* THE LONG GAME?

Business leader Gary Vaynerchuck has done a lot to popularize the idea of "playing the long game" in recent years. Let's take a look at his story to get a better sense of what the long game is and how it's played.

FROM HUMBLE BEGINNINGS

It's not far-fetched to say Gary Vaynerchuck was born an entrepreneur. As a kid, he ran eight different lemonade stands and stopped by each one at the end of the day to collect the profits. Then he got into trading baseball cards at tradeshows, where he'd make a couple thousand dollars every weekend.

At age fourteen, Vaynerchuck joined the family retail wine business selling wine at his dad's store. When he began, the company was valued at about $3 million. By 2005, he'd transformed it into a $60 million franchise.

To accomplish this, he created what he called the Wine Library. Through a series of YouTube videos, he positioned himself as an expert, as a guy who knows wine and knows how to help customers find the right wine for them. The idea worked, and it revolutionized the business.

Vaynerchuck could have stayed on with the company and

grown that success, but that wasn't his long game. So, he pivoted and started a $100 million media agency and has become one of the most influential entrepreneurs for the younger generation of professionals.

Today, he has millions of followers. He writes best-selling books. Everywhere he goes, he talks about the hustle of the long game, about the amount of work he has put in—literally since he was a kid—to generate the kind of success he's had.

GET YOUR HANDS DIRTY

At its core, Vaynerchuck's message is simple: whatever looks like an overnight success to the rest of the world was actually a decades-long commitment and longer to a long-term goal.

His driving philosophy is something Vaynerchuck calls "Clouds & Dirt." To him, "You need a healthy dose of those extremes: the clouds—the high-end philosophy of what you believe—and the dirt—the low-down subject matter expertise that allows you to execute against it. Forget about everything else."[23]

---

23 Gary Vaynerchuck. "Ignore Everything Between the Clouds and Dirt." *Gary Vaynerchuck.* (2015). https://www.garyvaynerchuk.com/ignore-everything-between-the-clouds-and-dirt/

If anyone lives this philosophy, it's Gary. Others may only see the clouds, those aspirational moments that make people like him fun to follow. But make no mistake, the man has unbelievable hustle. He puts out content constantly. He's always got a new book in the works.

To Gary Vaynerchuck, it's all about getting dirty, hustling, putting out fires, and winning on small bets—but never losing sight of the long game.

I knew I wasn't going to be running the world at twenty-three or twenty-four years old. I know I'm not going to be running the world at forty either. However, I know what I want five, ten, twenty, or more years from now. I know what it will take to get there, and despite those short-game misfires like the one in Gastonia, all of us at Fans First are full steam ahead.

SHARE YOUR LONG GAME

When you stare up at the clouds, share what you see. Inspire others. Many of the greatest business leaders do this.

Gary Vaynerchuck wants to buy the New York Jets. He landed in New York as an immigrant and has been a giant Jets fan ever since. By his reckoning, he's still got another twenty or thirty years of work ahead of him to make ownership a reality.

- Facebook cofounder Mark Zuckerberg tells anyone who asks that he's only 1 percent done with his mission—even after registering one-sixth of the world's population on Facebook! All his company's investments and long-term decisions follow from this mindset.

- Elon Musk has two successful companies, SpaceX and Tesla. But is that enough for him? Nope. He wants to get humankind to Mars, and he's set up a series of time-stamped benchmarks to get there.

- Amazon founder Jeff Bezos is always talking about day one. Never mind that Amazon is over twenty years old and is one of the most valuable companies in the world. Never mind that they dominate the online retail industry (and every other industry they touch). They're three chess games ahead of everyone else, because they continue to operate like a hungry startup.

It takes incredible courage to put your dreams out there, but it makes them more real. It pulls people into the conversation who might be able to help. You've still got to do the work yourself—as Vaynerchuck says, no one can grow his wealth enough to buy the Jets but him—but you can still enlist others in service of that goal.

THE THREE PS

What do you need to keep yourself working the dirt, keeping yourself accountable, and making things grow? In my experience, it all comes down to the three P's—patience, persistence, and perseverance.

PATIENCE

On the back of the Fans First Playbook, it says, "Be patient in what you want for yourself, but be impatient in how much you give to others."

But what does that mean, exactly?

It's easy to be impatient with the things we want for ourselves. But when we have big goals, impatience doesn't work.

You can't be impatient with the idea of getting on the cover of *Fortune*. You can't be impatient with the idea of building a multimillion-dollar company. You can't work on it for a day and call it good. You have to work on it every day for *years*.

That takes patience. In the meantime, while you're playing your long game, don't get lost in yourself. Give back to others. Do it eagerly, and do it often.

This is impatience as a positive. When you have the opportunity to give, don't settle for *not* giving. Expect the best out of yourself, and expect it immediately.

PERSISTENCE

We focus on giving to others at Fans First because we believe in the power of building relationships. This takes time. In both Gastonia and Savannah, reaching out to and connecting with different businesses and communities has taken me years—and I'm still not done.

For us, persistence means proving our mission to our communities continually. "Fans first, entertain always" can't be mere words. We have to back them up.

It's not always easy to do this. However, it's essential that we show up and be accountable regardless of the circumstances.

In our first year in Savannah, we went to a neighborhood association meeting near Grayson stadium. Much to our surprise, our announcement that one of our first games had sold out was met with backlash. I can still remember some of the comments:

"They never sold out games before!"

"This is a joke. You don't care about people."

"We live in this neighborhood. How dare you!"

"You should leave tickets for us!"

Hearing all of this sucked. I would have gladly been anywhere else in that moment. However, they were my neighbors, my community. As unreasonable as they may have sounded, I had to listen and be accountable.

Besides, while it may have been tough to see when I was being yelled at, their broader point was important: the community *wanted* to be a part of the festivities, but they felt like they were missing out. There was opportunity there. All I had to do was keep working at it.

PERSEVERANCE

In the business of long-term goals, you must be stubborn. You can't let the flops, the hard times, or the money stand in the way of your big picture.

When our all-you-can-eat fireworks night fizzled at Gastonia because we only brought in three grills, we didn't pack it in for the season.

We still had our long-term goal. But first, we had to take our lumps, talk about what happened, and refocus.

In baseball, once in a while you have to wear it. Sometimes that means you have to take a ball in the back, but you do it to help the team in the long run. Promotions are going to fail. Plans are going to fizzle. Fans are going to complain. Whatever the case, it's up to you to step up to the plate and let yourself get drilled.

THE INEVITABLE TOUGHNESS OF IT ALL

As I explained in the intro way back at the beginning of the book, when the Savannah Bananas began, there were some nonbelievers. We struggled to get the proper buy-in from our community, and while it wasn't very much fun, it was worth it.

Yep, things are going to get tough. Nothing wrong with that. The harder things get, the harder you've got to work to make sure you come out on top. Here are a few things I've learned in the course of my own game.

THE LONG GAME IS ONGOING

Success in one goal leads to challenges with the next.

The neighborhood association wasn't the only one upset when we began selling out. We have to refund fans every game because they can't find a seat.

High demand is a good problem to have, but it's still a problem. Further, our ability to solve that problem affects us both in the short-term and long-term.

Here's why. My long-term goal is to change the game of baseball. I want to take what a hundred thousand fans see every year in Savannah and share it with millions of more people. However, to do that, I have to live up to my own mission and take better care of the fans who come out every night.

WHAT THE LONG GAME TELLS ME

Being turned away because the game is sold out is not a Fans First experience. Being unable to find a seat is not a Fans First experience. Waiting in line an hour for food is not a Fans First experience.

If we're playing the long game, we have to understand how we can accommodate everyone who shows up—and even the people who don't. The long game says refunding tickets and offering apologies isn't enough.

Perhaps the solution is adding more seats (which we've

already done...*twice*). Perhaps it's adding an immersive digital component. It's up to us to find an answer so we can continue to serve more fans in more communities than we are—and *better* than we are.

SOMETIMES SH*T HAPPENS

I was at the concourse in the middle of a game, doing my yellow tux thing, when a gentleman came up to me and said, "Where's your bathroom?" Happy to help, I put my arm around him and showed him the way.

Little did I know that as we were walking, the poor man had the runs. All over the concourse.

Emily and Keke immediately sprang into action, happily (well, calmly anyway) cleaning up the mess with big smiles on their faces. The fans never noticed a thing.

To be clear: it was *a lot* of poop, and it smelled terrible. That poor man's bowels had more movements than a symphony. The best part is after the man emerged from the restroom, he went right back to his seat as if nothing had ever happened.

Here's the moral of the story. One, I had to get it into the book somehow, mostly because it's funny. Two, sh*t *is* going to happen. It just is. In our case, it literally happened.

When it happens, it's how you deal with it that matters most. We know what the Fans First long game is all about. We knew that the best thing to do was just clean it up and have a good laugh about it.

We didn't complain, hesitate, or react negatively in any way. If we had, I'm sure plenty of fans would have noticed. Then it wouldn't have just been our problem, but a few hundred other people's as well.

FOR YOUR VIEWING PLEASURE

It's nearly impossible not to laugh at a story of a grown man pooping his pants in public. Poop is funny, plain and simple.

Kmart would appear to agree. As proof, I submit to you this classic commercial. With one watch, you too may "ship your pants" (YouTube keywords: "Kmart ship my pants").

THE NETFLIX STORY

In 2010, Netflix's Reed Hastings was named CEO of the year. In 2011, he split the company in two—a DVD side of the company and a streaming side of the company. It caused chaos. Hastings quickly became known as the biggest idiot in Silicon Valley, and Netflix stock dropped from $300 to $60.

People are still writing think pieces about Netflix's folly. However, from Hastings's perspective, he was thinking about the long game. The decision he made may have caused him to look like an idiot, but time has shown it was the best decision for his company.

DVDS ARE THE PAST

Hastings knew that everyone loved DVDs, and Netflix was killing it with their mail service. However, Hastings also knew that streaming was the future. They had to retrain their customers or risk becoming obsolete. If that meant raising the cost of that service by 60 percent, then so be it.

In the short term, Netflix lost tons of subscribers and lost money for its investors. These days, however, Netflix is stronger than ever, offering original content like *House of Cards, Stranger Things*, and *Making a Murderer* that their fans can't stop talking about.

Reed Hastings understood what his core business is: entertainment and convenience, giving people creative content easier and quicker. He believed in what he was doing and had the vision of what Netflix could be best at—a different mindset.

This eye on the long game paid off. All those subscribers they lost came back—and then some. Because Hastings had his eye on the streaming content game, he beat companies like Amazon, Hulu, and Comcast to the punch. He had to take a hit to get there, but he was willing to gamble the entire company on that vision.

YOU GOTTA PUT IN THE WORK

In Tom Asacker's book, *The Business of Belief*, he discusses the concept of the power and strength of belief. In this journey of you as a reader, entrepreneur, and business owner—once you become a sponge, and then learn and realize what you can be best at, having mirror moments, simplifying and taking small steps—it's much easier to know what you believe in and use every moment to work toward it.

The idea of the long game is about putting in the necessary work. All the work you've put in to simplify, to make short-term wins for the long term—that's the work that will create the best success in the future.

When you get started, you can say, "I believe we are going

to be the best at this." Great. No arguments here. Be the best and set a long-term goal. It's not going to happen tomorrow or the day after.

START THAT JOURNEY

At twenty-three, I didn't know exactly what kind of journey I'd set out on. I had no idea I'd be leading a baseball circus. But just as I do today, I believed in my mission and long-term goals, and I knew that if we stuck to them, we could have a tremendous impact.

For you, the reader, this is key. This journey is something that will break you down and build you up. There will be tough times. There will be times you can do nothing but go bananas.

However, every time there's a flop, and every time you pick yourself back up, you're taking another step toward creating something magical. As we'll discuss in the next chapter, some of those steps are bigger than others. Sometimes, you have to go all-in.

THE YELLOW TUXOMETER

Here are some more yes or no questions for you. Give yourself ten points for yes, and one point for no.

1. Would your friends or spouse describe you as patient?

2. When you watch a TV show, do you complete the season or series?

3. Have you been with your current job for more than five years?

4. When you want something, will you do anything to get your way?

THE YELLOW TUX BOOKSHELF

Look, AC/DC said it best, "It's a long way to the top if you wanna rock and roll," or in this case, if you wanna yellow tux your business. The way I figure it, if you wanna get to the top, you gotta figure out where the top is and chart your path forward. Trust me, these books will help.

- *The Dip,* by Seth Godin

- *Crush It and Crushing It,* by Gary Vaynerchuck

- *Perennial Seller,* by Ryan Holiday

- *Customer Satisfaction Is Worthless,* by Jeffrey Gitomer

- *Take the Stairs,* by Rory Vaden

- *Living Forward,* by Michael Hyatt

CHAPTER *Eight*

GOING ALL-IN

Whenever you see a successful business, someone once made a courageous decision.

—PETER DRUCKER

When you're a business owner, the day will come when you have to lay it all out on the line.

If you believe in your mission and what you're doing, you'll gladly rise to the challenge. You won't doubt it for a second.

It's an incredible conviction, and it's what this chapter is all about. Behind every successful entrepreneur is an all-in moment—or two, or three.

Success always entails risk. Small steps are crucial, but they're not everything. Eventually, you're going to have to trust yourself, your business, and take a big leap to reach the top.

THE NUTS AND BOLTS OF GOING ALL-IN

All-in moments have a way of presenting themselves when it's time. Usually, it's after you've taken some important steps, seen what works, and had some wins.

At that point, the all-in moment will call you to do something big, something you've never done. It may be uncomfortable and scary, but it's worth it.

HOW DO YOU KNOW WHEN IT'S TIME?

The all-in moment is less a science and more of a feeling. As you'll see in my own story later, sometimes the signs are obvious. Other times, they're more subtle, but just as important.

In my experience, the telltale sign of the all-in moment is when someone asks, "Is it worth it?"

Usually, you already know the answer: *yes*.

When you believe in your business and what you're doing, you meet the all-in moment without a second thought.

You're ready to put in the work, regardless of what it might take.

In that way, while these all-in moments are incredibly important, they're also matter-of-fact. You know what you have to do, you know what you *want* to do, and now it's just a matter of doing it.

BELIEF AIN'T PASSIVE

You'll be amazed at what you're capable of, and what you're willing to endure, when you believe in something. If that means selling your house and couch-surfing as you try to establish a new business in a new city, so be it.

In this way, belief isn't passive. It's not a cheer you perform from the sidelines. It's something you do when you're in the thick of it all. For my wife and me, that meant going tens of thousands of dollars in debt, living in a crappy duplex, and throwing everything else on a platter to say, "This is what I can give, and it's everything."

WHO'S COMING WITH ME?

Remember way back in Chapter 1 when we talked about Jerry Maguire and his mirror moment? Well, after he was fired, he had no choice but to go all-in on his mission statement.

As he stood there defeated, about to walk out of his office, he looked around and said, "Who's coming with me?"

The all-in moment is an unbelievable rallying cry for others, whether friend, family, coworkers, or even yourself.

When we committed to creating the Bananas, we thought we had worked hard before. However, we didn't know what it was like to put everything we had into something. It was overwhelming at times, but we refused to fail.

Everyone around us noticed. When our president saw the huge financial risks we were taking, he was devastated, but inspired. He vowed to do everything he could to help, and he rallied the troops for our cause.

For many of our staff, this was their first job. They didn't know what it was like to be part of a vision that was larger than them. But when they saw the lengths we were willing to go to take things to the next step, a new culture was born.

If we were going all-in, they were going to go all-in too. Everyone knew the challenges, they knew no money was coming in, and they knew the Savannah community wasn't supporting our efforts yet. They didn't care. And together, we set out to prove the naysayers wrong.

IT'S BIGGER THAN YOU

Why did everyone rally for our cause? Because we never made the success of our business about us.

The predominant mindset in the business world is to maximize your returns for personal gain. These kinds of business people ask, "How can I make more?" when they should be asking how they can make more for others.

No all-in moment is a sure thing. However, you'll dramatically tip the scales in your favor when you invest in your business not for yourself, but for your people. Show them you're in it together, and they will move mountains for you when all the chips are on the table.

SMALL BETS EQUAL PROOF OF CONCEPT

We weren't blank slates when we arrived in Savannah. We proved in Gastonia that we could build something from nothing. Sure, Savannah was a larger market with a larger stadium, but we were ready to meet that challenge.

You want another way to improve your odds? Use your

small bets as a testing ground. Play the long game, make small bets, and prove the concept. Trust the experience. Even if your small bets only offer a glimmer of hope for success, that glimmer will make it a lot easier to push your chips in when the time comes.

WHAT IF IT DOESN'T WORK?

You go all-in. You fail. You're left with nothing.

Doesn't get scarier than that, does it?

Let's skip the motivational speeches here. Success entails risk. Failure is part of it.

Sometimes you're going to fail. But, hey, at least you'll be in good company. Walt Disney failed plenty of times. He lost his first studio in Kansas City—including the rights to his first creation, Oswald the Rabbit.

Disney even failed after he'd previously seen success. *Fantasia*, for instance, was considered a flop for years after its release. It didn't matter. Disney stuck with his vision, trusting that he would win more than he failed.

EYES ON THE LONG-TERM VISION

Even if you fail, going all-in can lead to a better future. At the minimum, it's a learning experience. The best success stories are full of failures. If you believe in what you're doing, it's rare you will fail and be unable to build yourself back up.

That's why having a long-term vision is so important. Gary Vaynerchuck wants to own the New York Jets, but it's going to take a few more all-in moments to get there. I want to be able to entertain millions of people a day, and it's going to take a lot more than what I'm doing now for that to happen.

When you have your long-term vision, you're constantly asking yourself how to get to the next stage. Sometimes, the only way to do that is to go big.

GO ALL-IN, THEN GO ALL-IN AGAIN

No career is marked by a single all-in moment. Succeed or fail, you're going to have to go all-in to keep pushing the boundaries of animation, to own the New York Jets, or to impact more lives.

I fully trust I will be going all-in again with Fans First Entertainment. It doesn't scare me. It's exciting. It gives me a sense of purpose, the opportunity to reinvent and create new things. I'll take that any day over playing it safe.

BANANAS OR BUST

You ready for the story of the big all-in moment for Fans First Entertainment?

Okay, so it began August 4, 2014. After a successful stint as GM, I was now the proud owner of the Gastonia Grizzlies. Things were going well—so well, in fact, that on this night, in front of a sold-out crowd, I asked the woman of my dreams to become my wife. Here's how it all went down.

HOW DO YOU KEEP FIREWORKS A SECRET?

All summer, I had planned on proposing on the last game of the year. It was going to be a big spectacle. I got both Emily's family and my family involved. We planned a secret fireworks show, which was basically an impossible task, but somehow we pulled it off.

I meant to propose at the end of the game, preferably after a big Grizzlies win. But then our pitcher allowed nine runs in the first inning, and things slowed to a crawl.

By the sixth inning, I couldn't take it anymore. It was time for a delay of my own.

As Emily was in the concessions stand making popcorn, I yelled over, "Hey, I'm taking all the staff onto the field for a promotion."

"Jesse, I'm right in the middle of popping popcorn!" she shouted over her shoulder.

"It doesn't matter," I said. "We need to get *everyone* on the field right now!"

Finally, she agreed. Everyone got on the field, we did our bit, and I thanked all the staff, except Emily.

Then it was time for the big moment.

"Last but not least," I said, looking over at her, "I'd like to thank our Director of Fun, Emily McDonald."

I stepped in front of her and faced the crowd. "Not many of you know this, but Emily and I met for the first time right here on this field." I explained a little bit more about our first encounter, then said, "Emily, in front of my family, your family, and our entire baseball family, will you make me the luckiest guy in the world?"

I dropped to a knee, produced a baseball, and opened it to reveal a ring.

Everything went in motion. Emily ran over to me and I took her into my arms. The fireworks started going off. The fans went crazy.

After a few minutes, the fireworks petered out, and we walked off the field. The umpires came back out. The Grizzlies took their positions, and the game resumed.

In all the excitement, Emily never even got to say "yes" to the proposal.

A TRIP TO SAVANNAH

A couple of days later, Emily unveiled a little surprise of her own: a weekend getaway to Savannah. We fell in love with the city immediately. The culture, the food, the views—all of it was perfect.

Then we took in a game at Grayson Stadium. It was a perfect summer night for a ball game at a picturesque ballpark, but there was no one there and no one seemed to care. This all but confirmed the rumblings that Grayson's current occupants would be leaving soon, leaving Savannah without a baseball team for the first time in decades.

While at the game, I texted the commissioner of the Coastal Plain League and said, "If the other team goes, we're taking their place." I don't know why exactly, but in that setting, in that stadium, and with that culture, I knew I could bring Savannah something it had never seen before. And over the next year, we worked day and night to make it happen.

ALL OR NOTHING

Our reckoning came in January 2016. We were at my college roommate's wedding when my wife got the phone call—we had overdrawn our account. Our bank account was zeroed out. We were broke.

Driving home the next day, Emily turned to me and solemnly said, "We have to sell our home."

That was that. End of discussion. Whatever it took to get the Bananas off the ground, we would do it.

We emptied our savings accounts. We sold our house. We got extra credit cards. We did *everything* to keep Fans First floating.

THE SADDEST-LOOKING DUPLEX EVER

With the little bit of money we held onto, we bought a small duplex on Tybee Island—though it certainly wasn't our first choice.

The six-hundred-square-foot home had been on the market for two years. The current resident's cats were the primary occupants. It smelled terrible. Its layout was odd. You couldn't even sit on the toilet without a few contortions.

I took one step inside that place and walked right back out.

Emily followed me out and stopped me. Just like she had done at my old roommate's wedding, she looked me in the eyes and said, "Jesse, there's nothing else."

We made an offer that day.

Soon, the duplex was ours. There was no turning back now. We had gone all-in on the Savannah Bananas. Our only choice was to see this crazy scheme through.

DIVE-BOMBING COCKROACHES? NO, THANK YOU

I'd love to tell you that with your all-in moment comes a sudden, life-changing moment of clarity. But I don't want to lie to you.

Instead, you get other moments. The night a cockroach landed on my head. The days ants showed up from nowhere and occupied *everywhere*. The nights spent balancing bowls of ramen on an inflatable mattress as we tried to live on less than a hundred dollars a week.

Most nights, we slept fitfully. One of us would wake up, walk around alone outside, and then get back into bed. Of course, since it was an air mattress, every time one of us got back in, the sudden weight shift would launch the other person toward the ceiling.

We had given everything to the Bananas, but so far, we had nothing to show for it. Even our all-in money was gone.

EVERY DECISION IS A BIG ONE

On February 25, 2016, we finally announced the Savannah Bananas to the world, and everything began to change. We were the number-one trending topic on Twitter. We received coverage on national media outlets. Our tickets began selling out, and so did our merchandise.

You already heard the story of our big unveiling in the Introduction. Instead of rehashing that, let's talk about how easily it could have gone the other way.

In your all-in moments, every decision is a big one. For us, perhaps no other decision was bigger than coming up with our name. We could have played it safe, but a safe name wouldn't fit for a brand that was going all-in on entertainment and fun. We needed a name that would match our particular brand of mayhem.

So, in November 2015, we reached out to the community.

All we asked was that they give us names that were different, unique, and fun. We knew if we were going to do something outrageous, we needed our community to get in the same mindset.

On the very first night of the contest, a woman named Lynn Moses submitted the name *Bananas*. We knew immediately that she'd picked the winner.

In total, we received nearly a thousand suggestions. No one suggested Bananas but Lynn. In fact, a lot of the suggestions were pretty run-of-the-mill: *Spirits*, *Seagulls*, *Anchors*, and *Ghosts*. Some people even suggested we stick with the previous team's name of *Sand Gnats*—which, trademark issues aside, there was no way we were going to do that.

Lynn got what we were going for right away. When we

asked her later why she suggested Bananas, her reasoning was perfect. She simply said, "Well, you said you guys wanted to be different, unique, and crazy, so I just thought Bananas!"

From there, we ran with it—because that's what you do when you go all-in. If we were going to be the Bananas, then we had to *go* bananas. This mindset gave rise to the Banana Nanas (our grandma dance team), the Banana in the Pants promotion, and banana beer.

With our Bananas brand and our unusual fan experience, we were introducing two things that the city of Savannah had never seen before. Fans could have easily said, "Screw this. I don't understand it. It's not what I'm accustomed to, and I'm not going to support it."

Instead, we succeeded because we knew our brand, we knew what we were about, and we committed to it 100 percent.[24]

DISNEY'S "FOLLY"

Walt Disney's life and career is full of moments of incredible patience, persistence, and perseverance (remember

---

24 And after a little pep talk from our coach, so did the players (YouTube keywords: "Savannah Mighty Bananas").

those three P's?) where he put those words directly into action.

Disney went from a studio in Kansas City, to a larger studio in Hollywood, to an even larger studio in Burbank, to a theme park in Anaheim, and to an entire city in Florida. At each point, he took small steps in pursuit of a bigger vision, followed by an all-in moment to reach the next level.

THE VISION: FULL-LENGTH FEATURES

Short films like the famous *Steamboat Willie* (which launched Mickey Mouse's animated career) marked Disney's first real successes. Each cost about $23,000 and netted his studio a profit.

Disney was happy with the success with short films, but he had a bigger vision: full-length, animated features. Unfortunately for him, such a venture wasn't even on anyone's radar in the 1930s. The staffing and production costs alone made it unthinkable for anyone besides him.

THE ALL-IN MOMENT

Uncle Walt believed in his vision. He wasn't going to give up just because it was challenging. He was going to put everything he had into making his vision a reality with the movie *Snow White and the Seven Dwarves*.

First, he bet his whole studio, the mortgage on his house, and everything else he had to find the $500,000 he estimated in production costs. That got the production started, but eventually, he realized he needed more. So, he went to Bank of America, played some early clips of the film, and refused to leave until the loan officer finally said, "All right, we'll invest in this."

The financiers weren't the only ones he had to sell his vision of *Snow White* to. Even his animators needed assurance. So, he gathered them in a room and put on a four-hour performance. He played all the characters himself with tremendous passion and bravado, demonstrating how great the story could be. By the end, the whole team was on board.

THE NARRATIVE SHIFT

It took three years and 750 animators to produce Snow White. In the meantime, Disney may have had the banks and the animators on his side, but the rest of the world was another story. Before seeing a single frame, the public called *Snow White* "Disney's folly." No one believed it could succeed—largely because nothing like it had ever been attempted.

By the time *Snow White* was released, Disney had spent about $1.5 million on the project (about $25 million today). If it failed, he would have lost everything, and today's massive entertainment empire would have been a flash-in-the-pan studio, more famous for its biggest blunder than anything else.

Fortunately for Disney, that's not what happened. *Snow White and the Seven Dwarves* brought in $8.5 million in its initial run. Today, it's recognized as one of the most successful films in history. Not only that, it opened up a whole new moneymaker for studios—animated films.

SHARE YOUR STORY

Disney succeeded not only because he believed in his vision, but also because he was an expert at sharing it with others—first with the banks, then with his animators, and finally with the public.

Part of his brilliance was that he didn't care if people thought he was crazy. With so many talking about his so-called folly, he knew people were interested. He knew they would buy a ticket just to see what all the fuss was about. And he also knew that once he had them in the theater, they would understand his vision.

A big part of entrepreneurship is making people care. Don't be the tree that falls in the forest when no one else is around. Make a sound. Announce yourself to the world.

As you'll see in the next chapter, it's amazing how you can control your destiny when you become a champion of your own story.

In our early days in Savannah, we knew we were struggling. We were broke, no one knew who we were, and the wheels were about to fall off the wagon.

However, no one else knew this. To the outside world, we were a team ready to make a splash, a business confident about who we were and what we could do. a can't-miss circus that everyone was invited to.

If we didn't get a little crazy and dare to share our story with the world, going all-in wouldn't have mattered. In the next chapter, you'll learn how to turn heads when you're ready to hit the big stage.

THE YELLOW TUXOMETER

For each question, answer with one of the following: all the time (ten points), sometimes (five points), or never (one point).

1. How often are you doing work that you believe in?

2. How often is the vision of your company shared by you or with you?

3. I think about my customers more than my product. (Yes: ten points; No: one point.)

4. How often do you envision a better life for yourself?

5. How often do you write down your goals to achieve a better life?

THE YELLOW TUX BOOKSHELF

This wouldn't be a business book if I didn't quote the great Wayne Gretzky, "You miss 100 percent of the shots you don't take." It's cliché, but it's true. And that's what going all-in is all about. Here are some books that will help you on your way (and whose titles are definitely not euphemisms).

- *The Obstacle Is the Way*, by Ryan Holliday

- *Pour Your Heart Into It*, by Howard Schultz

- *Screw It, Let's Do It*, by Richard Branson

- *Zero to One, by Peter Thiel*

- *The Hard Thing about Hard Things*, by Ben Horowitz

- *So Good They Can't Ignore You*, by Cal Newport

Part III

YELLOW TUXING
YOUR LEGACY

CHAPTER *Nine*

HELLO, WORLD

Without promotion, something terrible happens...nothing.

—P.T. BARNUM

Once you're all-in, it's time to make the world notice. Especially in the beginning, that leaves you with only one thing to do—promote like crazy.

It's the only way to announce yourself to the world, to say, "Hello, everyone. This is what I'm doing. I'm pretty excited about it, and I want to share it with you."

When you get ready for your big "Hello, world" moment, there are tons of questions:

- What are you going to do to stand out?
- What do you want everyone talking about?

- How will you get people to take notice—locally, nationally, or globally?
- What makes your idea so different that people should stop, pay attention, and care?

There are plenty more questions, but here's the bottom line: never stop promoting. Create new opportunities to put yourself out there. People aren't going to find out about you all at once. It's up to you to keep the pressure on and give the world a dance to discover you and whatever crazy thing you're up to.

ANYONE CAN MAKE A SPLASH

Some companies go for the soft opening. Others just open without any fanfare and hope the business starts trickling in.

They say, "Well, we're just another insurance company. We're going to open on July 15."

That's it.

They don't try to differentiate themselves from other insurance companies. They don't try to make a splash. They simply open their doors and get to the boring business of explaining what they do to a disinterested clientele.

BE BRAVE

It doesn't matter if you're an insurance company or a law firm. You could be *the only* insurance company or law firm in the minds of everyone around you. All you have to do is open with something spectacular, something so outrageous that everyone will be talking about it.

But this means being brave. A lot of companies will say, "Well, I don't want to be in the middle of a spectacle. We'll just go about our business."

That's not a growth mindset. Instead, try thinking, "Hey, this is an *opportunity*! We're doing things differently. We have something special, and this is a great story. Let's share it!"

YOUR STORY EQUALS YOUR YELLOW TUX

The media is always looking for a good story. For Fans First, that means getting crazy with yellow tuxes and officiating rounds of musical toilets.

You don't necessarily need all that. What you need is to find *your* yellow tux—your unique story—which makes you stand out from everyone else.

Maybe someone in your office has a really offbeat story

about how they became a lawyer. Maybe an insurance agent used to be a *Baywatch*-style lifeguard before an incident at the beach made them realize the importance of personal insurance.

Every business has a thousand good stories. The question is, do you know what those stories are, and are you doing anything to share them?

THINK LIKE A REPORTER

If you want the world to notice, then you first need to understand what the world is curious about. You must put yourself into the shoes of a reporter. What type of story would they *want* to cover?

At Fans First, we're known for being different. That's a great thing, but it means we have to double our energy thinking of new ways to be crazy. Otherwise, the media has no reason to show up.

Remember that Blue Ocean strategy that Cirque du Soleil used so well? That extends to marketing too. If you're promoting things that aren't usually event-worthy, you're bound to turn some heads.

At least, that's what we're banking on when we unveil

our latest round of merchandise this fall. Usually, brands just put out the merchandise, throw a little blurb up on Facebook, and say, "Here, come buy some stuff."

Not the Bananas. We're going full Dolce & Gabbana—or should I say Dolce & Banana? That's the only way to give our new Bananas undies, which come in "little banana" and "big banana" sizes, the launch they deserve. After all, everyone knows that banana hammocks are classy, and nothing says classy like a black-and-white commercial with one of our staff members lounging on the mound in underwear while Italian music plays in the background.

When you're thinking like a reporter, you're essentially asking the question, "Why would anyone care?" No matter what you're planning, if you can't answer that question, you might wanna shift gears and try something else.

MAKE ROOM FOR THE UNEXPECTED

When the Bananas said hello to the world, we thought of every banana-related thing we could do to get the media's attention.

We unveiled the name and logo during a big to-do at Grayson Stadium. We unveiled our mascot, Split (the King of Potassium), at an elementary school in front of thousands of kids a few weeks later. We were strategic with every little item, and it worked.

However, some of the best stories you can't plan for—and that's a good thing.

One of our ticket salespeople didn't plan on finding an abandoned puppy outside of our office. We did everything to find her proper home, but with no tags and no one claiming her, we brought her into the fold as Bat Dog.

We wanted to announce Bat Dog to the world, but even then, we didn't think it was a big story. So, we kept it small, had a photographer take some pictures, and sent out a release.

The story went viral immediately, gaining us more media attention than anything else we'd done before. We were surprised by our good fortune, but maybe we shouldn't have been. After all, who doesn't like a story about a rescued puppy?

The big lesson for us was to embrace new storytelling opportunities—especially the ones you don't plan. Often, the ones that drop into your lap have the best chance of becoming something special.

THE LITTLE STORIES REINFORCE THE BIG STORIES

Another reason the Bat Dog story resonated so well was it reinforced the larger story we were trying to tell. I've found this is a common thread in organizations that are good at standing out. They know how to find the story in everything, no matter how big or how small.

This goes hand in hand with our "If it's normal, do the exact opposite" philosophy. Not everything is going to create national attention. However, just like with Bat Dog, any story has the potential to become something bigger.

Even if a particular story doesn't explode, it reinforces what you're all about. Of course, our ticket takers are dressed up like bananas. Why wouldn't they be? That's who we are!

BE WHO YOU *WANT* TO BE

Remember back in Chapter 2 when I asked you to think about what business you're *actually* in? There's no better time to draw that distinction than when you're announcing yourself to the world.

The Gastonia Grizzlies and the Savannah Bananas play baseball. However, we're an entertainment company. Baseball is only a small piece of what we do.

Our marketing always reflects that. We celebrate our team, our players, and our coaches all the time. We give our fans plenty of reasons to love and appreciate all the great people who take the field for us each night.

However, we celebrate from an *entertainment* perspective, not from a baseball perspective. We don't make much noise about wins and losses or having the best pitchers and hitters in the league. That won't draw fans to the games—but the show will.

Every company can learn how to make that distinction. Sure, your insurance company can brag about breaking the record for most claims, but is that the reason people want to do business with you?

Look carefully at what aspect of your business you're promoting—and what you're ignoring. If it's the same thing as everyone else, then you're not sharing what makes you stand out. You're repeating what you think people want to hear rather than what *you* want to share.

BE REPEATABLE

Great leaders are repeatable. They'll repeat themselves over and over and over again. Once your fans and the media begin repeating you and the message you're trying to send to the world, you know you've created a positive chain of promotion.

Earlier in 2017, MSNBC visited Savannah to do a feature on the Bananas. They wanted to find out more about what we have going on down here. In the very first clip they aired, I heard the producer repeating one of our favorite talking points. "It's a real circus, and then a baseball game breaks out," she said. "You've never seen anything like this."

This is one of our talking points for a reason. We know it makes a good story. We know the media likes talking about people doing a one-eighty from the norm. By repeating phrases like this, we help them capture our story in a way that creates a story.

These talking points are how you get people interested. But remember, actions are repeatable too—and they're an essential part of your story. If you *say* you're fans first, for instance, you'd better be prepared to back that up every day.

TAKE CARE OF THE FANS

Let me tell you a story about one of our sponsors. A while back, the owner casually mentioned to us that her big anniversary was coming up in the spring.

Marie, our servicing director, remembered the conversation and made a note. Once spring rolled around, Marie showed up to our sponsor's office with a bottle of wine and a small gift.

The owner was dumbfounded. "Why are you here?" she asked.

"It's your anniversary!" Marie said. "I just wanted to celebrate and congratulate you."

A few days later, we got a letter from her thanking us and saying, "You have no idea how much this means. You guys truly are fans first."

Our company name is literally Fans First Entertainment. All we talk about is putting the fans first. Letters like this are special for us, because they tell us we're doing our job and that others are sharing our story.

TAKE CARE OF THE MEDIA

It's your job to make fans out of everyone. That means making fans out of your employees, customers, and sponsors. It *also* means making fans out of the media. Don't worry about cost. After all, if you're playing the long game, it pays for itself.

We take care of the media at every one of our shows. If they're nice enough to come out and cover us, we want to at least be nice enough to offer them good seats, tasty food, and whatever else they might need to take in the atmosphere.

I've heard a lot of business owners say to me, "How come the media never covers me?"

To them, I always ask, "Well, what do you do for the media?"

The media is always looking for good stories. But you have to give them reason to come out. You have to share your platform with them. You have to take care of them, make them feel welcome, and say, "Hey, this is what we're doing, we think it's pretty special, and we'd love it if you shared it with others."

MARKETING VS. ATTENTION

What's more important to a business: marketing or attention?

If you were to ask Amazon, the answer would resoundingly be marketing. Amazon has literally thousands of books on marketing, but only a handful of books on attention.

Why? Simply put, marketing is sexy. Most people genuinely

believe marketing is the key to a business's success. Everyone wants to work in marketing, which is a good thing, since everyone wants to hire an army of good marketers.

Here's the thing—you can be the best marketer in the world, but if no one's paying attention, it's not going to amount to much. Attention must come first.

Remember those all-you-can-eat Bananas tickets I talked about in the last chapter? I'm still proud of this idea. The product is unreal, and the value is even better.

When we first came up with this new ticketing model, I marketed the heck out of it. I promoted it on social media, bought ad time on the radio, sent a slew of direct emails, and even made cold calls.

And then—crickets. We didn't sell a thing.

In retrospect, it's easy to see why nobody cared. Marketing push or not, we hadn't bothered to earn anyone's attention first.

We wouldn't get anyone's attention either until we announced the Bananas brand a few months later. Now that we had everyone paying attention and talking about the team, we ran the same marketing push again. This time, sales skyrocketed.

These days, I'm more interested in hiring attention-getters than marketers. I've found that if your business stays focused on gaining attention, the marketing will take care of itself.

And how do you get attention? Well, that's what finding your yellow tux is all about.

ARE YOU CRAZY ENOUGH?

What's the craziest thing you've done in the past year? What's the craziest thing your business has done?

Let me guess, the first question was a little easier. Maybe you did something nuts on a recent vacation or pulled a particularly inspired prank on your best friend from college.

That second question was probably a lot tougher, though, wasn't it? Not many people do crazy things with their business.

That's too bad. Adding a little crazy to the workday is a great way to get attention.

Just look at Lady Gaga and Miley Cyrus. I mean, they're no Jenny Lind (you'll understand this reference by the end of the chapter), but they're masters of change. From costumes to characters to musical styles, both reinvent themselves more often than I change the oil on my car. And it works. People are always waiting to see what crazy thing one of them is going to do next. Some complain about the new crazy thing, while others embrace it. Most importantly, no one's on the fence. Everyone's talking about it.

On the business side of things, services like Uber and Airbnb couldn't have existed ten years ago. No one would have imagined that a couple of taps on a smartphone would bring a cab directly to you within minutes. Let's not forget how crazy Airbnb sounds on paper. Who would have thought you could make a business out of staying in strangers' spare rooms? And yet, in both cases, that's how a good percentage of people get around these days.

Your crazy ideas don't need to be game changers like Uber or the iPhone. They just have to be unexpected.

IS IT SHAREABLE?

When you're crazy, you're also shareable. That's a big deal in our modern world of social media.

Everybody likes sharing. Sharing is social currency. And if you're good at it, you can make the world move with surprisingly little effort.

Marketers still struggle with this concept. They're busy putting out content that matters to them, but not to their audience. Just think about my big marketing push with our all-you-can-eat Bananas tickets. It didn': matter how much it mattered to me if people were asking more basic questions like, "Wait, who are you again?"

Think back to what your parents taught you when you were a kid: sharing is caring. If no one shares, no one cares.

To get the shares, your job is to add value. Ditch the salesy, marketing speak and simplify your message.

Be funny. Be entertaining. Be surprising. Be educational. Be whatever you want. Just make sure you're sharing for others' benefit and not your own.

HELLO A THOUSAND TIMES

If you've taken anything away from this book, I hope it's that you should be uniquely you. Being different creates intrigue and excitement. It gives people something to talk about when they get home.

We named our second baseball team the Savannah Bananas because we like to get a little crazy—and we wanted our new community to know that.

It has paid off great so far. No college team has ever sold out an entire season before us.

But as cool as that is, I'm all too aware that our success could be wiped away in a heartbeat if we don't continue to introduce ourselves to the world. We realize we have a responsibility every day, every year to do something bigger than the previous year.

EVERY STORY IS A SMALL BET

If you look at each small step as a marketing opportunity, you will always find ways to succeed and stand out.

Not everything the Bananas do is going to get national attention. Naturally, I would love it if we did, but the truth is that with a *small steps* mentality, we don't need every story to go viral.

With this mindset, our job is simple: keep putting new things out there, and eventually something will hit. It's not enough to put out one press release, to run one promotion, and be done with it.

Even the promotions that don't hit on a national level are still going to get some attention. If people are having fun, it's a win-win.

Besides, you never know what's going to catch on.

- When we made tuxedo jerseys with actual collars as our players' uniforms for the season, we certainly thought it might turn some heads. We didn't think it would end up on ESPN.
- When we offered the outgoing President Obama a summer internship with our ball club in 2017, we thought we were just being funny.[25] When the story found its way to both radio and newspaper, we saw how funny everyone else thought it was too.
- When we ran a beer fest, we started it at 9:00 a.m. just to see if anyone would show up. But with a slogan like, "You can't drink all day if you don't start in the morning," our fans couldn't resist the challenge.

Again, if it's normal, we do the exact opposite. And we do this by making small bets and seeing how they pan out. Each one has the potential to be a dynamite story—and many end up being exactly that. Sometimes, though, one of our brilliant ideas is bound to fizzle out.

---

25 It was pretty funny. See for yourself on YouTube (keywords: "Savannah Bananas Obama's Internship Offer").

THE INEVITABLE FIZZLE

A while back, we decided to have a boy band night in Gastonia. Since we didn't have the budget to bring the Backstreet Boys or One Direction, we figured we'd start our own boy band, the Claw City Boyz, instead.[26]

Armed with $75, the four members of Gastonia's finest pop group headed off to the local thrift store to assemble their costumes. One found a denim vest that he wore with no shirt, another one found some rockin' white pants, while one of the others fashioned his whole look around a fancy-looking glove.

Next, we filmed their debut music video on our stadium's rooftop, promoted them as the headliners of Boy Band Night, and set to work on their choreography. We laughed every step of the way, and we were sure it was going to be a big hit.[27]

The fans, however, were disappointed. They wanted a real boy band, not some locals playing dress-up. No one showed up to the game. We had less than five hundred fans that night.

---

26 Need a little hype music as you read through this section? I recommend some Backstreet Boys on YouTube (keywords: "Backstreet Boys Everybody Backstreet's Back").

27 Check out the Claw City Boyz in all their glory (YouTube keywords: "Gastonia Grizzlies Claw City Boyz Music Video").

None of that mattered to the Claw City Boyz. They still felt like celebrities. They did their dances, signed autographs for the few people who were actually interested, and ignored all the *boo birds*.

It was a total disaster from a promotional perspective, but it was also a great learning opportunity. Moments like that, combined with unexpected media frenzies generated by something like Bat Dog, began to paint a better picture in our minds of what works and what doesn't.

This isn't rocket science, but one thing we've certainly learned in all of this is that people love stories that are cute or heartwarming. So, if you have stories involving rescued puppies, dancing grandmas, or goofy wedding proposals, make sure your local media outlets know what's going on.

WITH THE FIZZLE COME THE CRITICS

You're always going to have your haters. There will always be people who don't believe in what you believe in. For instance, more traditional-minded baseball fans aren't always our biggest fans. We understand and respect that.

We know we're not above criticism. We even try to embrace it to whatever extent we can, though it takes some thick skin sometimes. If nothing else, at least our critics are paying attention. At least we've given them something to talk about.

Here's the thing, feedback is feedback. Sometimes great feedback comes from people who hate what you're doing. Other times, bad feedback comes from people who love what you're doing.

Either way, I've learned to take the feedback as a learning opportunity. When someone offers feedback, do they understand what we're trying to build? If not, why not? Are we living up to our Fans First promise? Are we reaching new audiences who are still learning what we're all about?

Henry Ford once said, "If I asked people what they wanted, they would have said faster horses." Not every bit of feedback is going to be useful. However, the better you get at announcing yourself to the world and controlling your story, the more others will engage you on *your* terms and offer more productive feedback.

THE MASTER SHOWMAN

P. T. Barnum is, without a question, one of my favorite role models. Why? Well, he was a genius at promotion and the quintessential American showman. He built an empire around a childlike sense of fun and adventure. Here are a couple of my favorite stories.

THE AMERICAN MUSEUM

In the 1840s, Barnum bought the American Museum in New York. He wanted to relaunch it as something spectacular, but it was going to take some heavy lifting. Crews worked through the night, hanging up giant plaques of animals all over the front façade. Then, he strung up flags from all over the world and hired one of the worst bands he could find to play out on the balcony.

That last bit is my favorite part. When people showed up for the big unveiling the next day, they all complained about the music. That's when Barnum pounced. "What do you expect for nothing?" he would reply.

The spectacle immediately got people talking. He put everything he had into launching that museum, awful band and all, and it worked.

People bought into this bizarre novelty because Barnum did. He sold it perfectly. Soon, thousands of people were paying their twenty-five cents to visit the museum every day, and it became one of Barnum's most profitable ventures.

JENNY LIND

One of my favorite Barnum stories has to do with the famous singer, Jenny Lind. Never heard of her? Don't worry, no one else had either until Barnum came around.

As the story goes, Barnum heard of this great singer in Europe named Jenny Lind. Sight unseen, he decided he wanted her to tour America as one of his performers.

Like Barnum, no one in the United States knew anything about her. To other promoters, this would have been a problem. However, to Barnum, this meant he could turn her into whatever he wanted. Lind may have been a good singer, but Barnum would make her a legend.

First, he paid thirty reporters to write stories about her—though never about her singing. Instead, he had them focus on everything else: her personality, her character, her celebrity in Europe, you name it.

He wanted people to be fascinated by her—and it worked. Soon, all of America was buzzing with anticipation over this unknown "it" girl. When Lind finally arrived from Europe, forty thousand people (who had never heard her sing) were there to greet her.

Barnum had created a celebrity out of thin air. Newspapers

would sell out simply because they printed her picture. Products including beds, pianos, hats, and chewing gum were rebranded and named after her. Everywhere she went, a crowd followed, and all her shows sold out.

Was she actually a good singer? As, it turns out, yes she was. By all accounts, she was amazing. But that wasn't really the point. Lind had already seen success, but Barnum found a way to make her a legend.

That's the power of a good "Hello, world" moment. Barnum had no idea his plan would work, but in a lot of ways, it was a small bet. He'd already seen success through the American Museum and other performers like General Tom Thumb. If Jenny Lind hadn't caught on, he would have been fine.

That said, by turning Jenny into a larger-than-life character, he invested in his success (and in hers). In doing so, he dramatically increased the chances that his little gamble would pay off.

THE LARGER-THAN-LIFE MENTALITY

Barnum made everything he touched seem larger than life. If it was bold, it was Barnum. If it was big, it was Barnum. This was no accident. As Barnum once said, "To make big money, I must always think and act in big ways."

Time and again, this philosophy paid off. He may not have had access to the marketing tools we enjoy today, but he knew how to work with what he had. From there, all it took was a little bravery.

Oh, and a lot of fun.

THE YELLOW TUXOMETER

Here are some more yes or no questions for you. Give yourself ten points for yes, and one point for no.

1. Has the media covered your story or the story of your business?

2. Have you done anything dramatically different with your business this year?

3. Do your social media posts get shared every time?

4. How often do you question whether it's even possible to do certain things with your business?

THE YELLOW TUX BOOKSHELF

It's time for you to channel your inner Adele and say, "Hello, it's me." Except maybe be a little happier about it. At any rate, when you're ready for your time to shine, you'd better be ready. These books will help you get there.

- *All Business Is Show Business*, by Scott McKain

- *Amazement Revolution*, by Shep Hyken

- *Stand Out*, by Dorie Clark

- *Magnetic*, by Joe Calloway

- *Pursuit of Wow*, by Tom Peters

CHAPTER *Ten*

FUN IS A PRIORITY

Fun is one of the most important and underrated ingredients in any successful venture.

—RICHARD BRANSON

Richard Branson is a legend. It's hard to think of Richard Branson without thinking about him doing something crazy. In fact, I've heard that Dos Equis's famous mascot, The Most Interesting Man in the World asks Richard Branson for advice.

Despite his image as a carefree playboy, Branson owns hundreds of businesses. Some have collapsed, some have rebounded from hardships, and some are thriving. Through it all, Branson has operated by one simple rule: have fun.

This ethos reflects in Branson's businesses. I remember

when my parents first flew Virgin Air. They couldn't stop raving. From the customer service to the seating, everything contributed to a sense of fun and adventure during their flight.

What's always stood out to me about that story is that my parents couldn't quite articulate what made flying Virgin so good. The most they could say was that I *had* to try it myself.

That's the same spirit we try to foster at a Grizzlies or Bananas game. I want the fun to be everywhere and apparent, but I want the experience to be difficult to put into words. There's nothing better than a fan telling another potential fan, "Just go. *You'll see* what I'm talking about."

ALL ABOARD THE FUN MACHINE

Want to know the secret to making fun a priority in your business? Make it a part of everything.

There are a lot of ways you can approach this, but the idea is simple. Start with your fans. Now ask yourself, for everything you do, for every touch point, is it fun for them? How does your staff answer the phone, and what is the voicemail like? How does the staff greet fans who come into the office? What do your fans think about the penguins?

Wait, penguins?

Okay, so maybe that last one was a little specific to us. One of the first things fans see when they drive into the ballpark at Grayson is penguins. Well, our Parking Penguins to be exact. Why? Well, because it's *fun*. Who doesn't like penguins? And who wouldn't like people dressed up as penguins to help you park your car?

WALKING THAT WALK

Here's another great thing about the penguins (and there are so many great things about penguins): it backs up our stated commitment to fun with living, breathing, squawking evidence.

Look, a lot of companies say fun is important to them. Take one look at their mission statement, however, and you won't find it anywhere. They may pay lip service to it, but it's abstract, something a manager might say during a Monday afternoon meeting. "Hey, have fun this week, everybody!"

In one of the great ironies of the world, telling someone to have fun is about the least fun thing you can do (and yes, I'm aware that I've dedicated a whole chapter to telling you to have fun). You have to *make* fun happen by infusing it into everything you do. Don't just talk that talk. Walk that walk.

DROP THE JARGON

You want to know another thing I like about fun? It's the opposite of jargon and empty marketing language that doesn't actually mean anything.

You ever see those companies that love to say they satisfy customers and exceed expectations?

You ever stop to think about what that means?

As soon as you tell people you exceed expectations, you don't. That's a promise you can't live up to. Your fans will always be expecting something slightly better because you told them you're better than they expected.

The same thing goes for customer satisfaction. What does that even mean?

If you're a business, why do you merely want to satisfy a customer? As a customer, why do you want to be merely satisfied? Do you ever come home and tell your spouse you had a satisfying day?

Satisfaction is average. It's not fun. All it means is that you did enough for your customers not to complain.

The companies that use language like this—customer satisfaction and exceeding expectations—end up chasing data points on a spreadsheet. As soon as you're committed to customer satisfaction, you're committed to customer satisfaction surveys.

And where is the fun in a customer satisfaction survey? Has *anyone* ever had a good time filling one out?

Forget the surveys. Do a great job, make fun a priority, and your fans will find plenty of ways to let you know.

A COMMITMENT TO FUN IS A COMMITMENT TO IDEAS

The great thing that happens when you change fun from an abstract concept to a specific, repeatable action, is you get more ideas.

You like ideas, right? I thought so.

Because we're committed to making everything fun, we *have* to think differently. That forces us to break down every step of our process and think about what can be done better than anyone else. After all, if you see the same thing over and over again, it stops being fun after a while.

That's why some of the most fun I have every day is when I get together with our videographer, director of entertainment, and marketing head to talk about our next batch of promotions. That's why I'm hyena laughing most days around two o'clock, literally bent over in stitches thinking about all the crazy things we just dreamed up.

I consider that just about a perfect day. Not only are we having the time of our lives, but we're coming up with new ways to entertain our fans. The more you're enjoying yourself, the more you're willing to turn your inner critic off and just let go, the more you're practicing the art of the good idea.

THERE IS NO FUN SWITCH

Fun takes practice. You or your office manager don't just turn on a fun switch and tell people to get crazy with it.

I'm sure we could have a lot of fun with such a switch if it existed, but it doesn't. You gotta work for your fun. You gotta earn it.

Want to know the best way to get in the business of having

fun? Get outside of your comfort zone. Surround yourself with different people and different experiences. Expand your normal sphere of influence and learn something new.

Grayson Stadium is now home to a whole host of theater and improv people because we embraced this mindset. I know very little about their world, and they know very little about ours. But they sure bring a lot to the table—and, *man*, do we have fun together.

The other day, one of our performers came up to me and said, "Why isn't this game over? Did it go into overtime?"

"It's baseball," I said. "It doesn't have overtime. But it *does* have extra innings."

"Okay, okay," he said walking away, still confused.

It's always hilarious when someone doesn't know the thing you know. But in this case, it also means I'm hiring the right people. If I brought people in who *liked* baseball, I'd be bringing in people accustomed to how the sport is played everywhere else—slow, long, and boring.

That's not what we're about. We're about entertainment. We're about fun. That means we need to be hiring people who are about entertainment and fun too.

So, forget the fun switch. Bring in fun, creative, and entertaining people. They'll bring in a whole new flavor of fun from the outside world that you weren't even aware of.

LOOSEN UP

Recently, I read a book called *Play It Away*. In it, author Charlie Hoehn talks openly about the general anxiety and panic attacks he would have from working so hard. Now, I don't know if you've ever had a panic attack before, but it's basically the opposite of fun.

Hoehn was tired of having the opposite of fun, so instead, he committed to actually *having fun*, and it changed his life. He didn't have to get crazy with it; he just started playing catch or going to the batting cages every day.

That's all it really takes to loosen people up. No need to force it. Just do what sounds good.

A lot of companies try to get too programmatic with the idea of fun. They go through the motions of fun by setting up a ping-pong table in the office. Sure, that *could* be fun, but if the office doesn't have any ping-pong players, that table is likely to go unused.

At Fans First, we embrace fun, but we let it rise out of our culture and what we already enjoy doing. I take walks around the ballpark with my staff all the time. Some of our staff hit the batting cages like Charlie Hoehn. Sometimes we all break out into an impromptu kickball game.

IS FUN IN THE OFFICE EVEN POSSIBLE?

Even at the Fans First office, we're not having fun all the time. In fact, during the first two weeks leading up to the 2017 season, we had all morphed into giant stress monsters, with the office as our battleground.

Our business had grown to new levels, and while we were rising to the challenge, our culture started to take a hit in the process. Luckily, we were able to step back and remind ourselves that fun wasn't just something we had during showtime. Fun was something we had *all the time*.

We kept working hard, but we remembered what made the office fun—the irreverent morning Snapchats, the ridiculous banter, the crazy things our fans say about us on social media that we read aloud to each other.

FUN MAKES YOU BETTER

Whatever gets us laughing doesn't merely get us through our days better. It makes us better at our jobs.

In a great TED Talk (and an even better book), speaker Shawn Achor called this the "happiness advantage." Through a series of Harvard studies, Achor found that the best-ranked students in their class weren't happy. Sure, they got good grades, but only in pursuit of a happiness that kept escaping them.

These students figured achievement would fill the happiness void, but Achor found the opposite was true. Those who were happy *to begin with* were more productive and successful.

I share this little tidbit with everyone at Fans First, be it the players or the staff. Yes, we have a job to do. Yes, we have to perform. However, if we don't have fun around each other, if we don't love what we're doing, none of the success happens.

Too many companies say they're going to do this or that to drive revenue. Only then are they allowed to have fun.

I say it doesn't work that way. Even Harvard studies say it doesn't work that way.

Make fun a priority, make it part of your culture, and watch the innovation, creativity, and success flow from you.

FANS FIRST FUNNING AROUND

Hanging on our office wall, we have the Fans First Way—which, in case you forgot, says, "Always Be Caring, Different, Enthusiastic, Fun, Growing, and Hungry."

We don't get this right 100 percent of the time. However, because we're committed to these values, even in our deepest funks, fun is usually right around the corner. Here are a couple of my favorite examples.

YOU NEVER KNOW WHEN A BALL GAME MIGHT BREAK OUT

One Saturday in 2017, we put on one of our best shows ever. We had an impromptu marriage proposal, the best-ever toddler vs. turtle race, and a legendary show by the Bananas Band. Everything went perfectly, and we were so charged up after the game that none of the staff wanted to leave.

So, we didn't. Instead, we played kickball under the Grayson Stadium lights until two in the morning, laughing and dancing to the music blaring over the PA system.

Some days later, our director of operations asked me what my favorite moment of the season had been so far.

Without hesitation, I answered, "Saturday night watching the entire staff play kickball into the early morning, listening to music, having fun. That was the best moment."

Most people would assume my favorite moment would have been something from one of our games or in-game promotions—the strike-out-cancer walk, the cruise giveaway, our tenth straight sellout, MSNBC spending a few days with us as they put together their feature story about the Bananas.

Those are all great. A lot of great things happen when you've professionally gone bananas.

But when it comes down to it, the moments that matter most are always my family at Fans First having the time of their lives. I would trade everything else to have that feeling every day, because I know the business and the culture we've built around it can only keep growing.

PUTTING FANS FIRST'S BIGGEST FANS FIRST

Let me tell you about Danny. This guy worked crazy hard to get a job with us. He emailed. He called. He was unbelievably persistent. He put everything he had into it. Eventually, we had no choice but to give him a job, even though we didn't have a job to give him.

It didn't matter. He saw what we were building and knew he had to be part of it. His first year, he worked with almost every community group, church, school, and kids' sports league in Savannah. Throughout the season, he was able to help to raise $41,000 for local nonprofits. What he accomplished on behalf of Fans First was nothing short of amazing. He was one of the biggest reasons we were able to impact so many fans our first season.

Danny is from Cleveland, and he and his dad are diehard Indians fans. So, when the Indians made the 2016 World Series, we knew we had a chance to do something special for him.

Naturally, we had to have a little fun with him too. So, the next day, in front of the whole staff, we gave him a gift of a toy airplane and said, "This represents how far you've come, how far you're taking us, and how everyone's jumped on the plane with you. Danny, we appreciate you."

Politely, Danny took the plane and said, "Oh, thanks."

Just as he was about to get back to work, I looked at him and said, "It also represents the fact that we're flying you to Game One of the World Series with your dad, and you leave tomorrow.

He got all choked up, thanked us, then called his dad—who was blown away. Soon, they were off in Cleveland for a once-in-a-lifetime opportunity.

That's what fun can build. That's what a culture based on trust and gratitude can create.

FISH ARE FUN

Did you know a fish market is the thirteenth most-visited place in the United States? Well, now you do.

Say hello to Pike's Place Fish Market in Seattle.

At first, the place was a flop. In his book, *When Fish Fly*, original owner Josh Yokoyama described the market's early days. He would yell at his employees. His employees would yell back. They would fight, get fired, or quit in an endless revolving door of workers. It wasn't an environment anyone wanted to be part of.

FROM FLOP TO FLIGHT

As this was going on, Yokoyama began working with a business coach. In the process, he learned that if he wanted to make the Fish Market better, he needed to instill happiness and fun into the workplace.

These days, Pike's Place Fish Market is a world-famous spectacle. Employees throw fish at customers. They try to resurrect other (often headless) fish on the countertops. They take photographs with anybody who asks. I have even seen a video of an employee chasing a group of tourists with a giant octopus.

It's insane, but people love it. Anyone who visits Seattle makes sure to pay the Fish Market a visit.

The Pike's Place Fish Market rose from a hostile, miserable workplace to a mega-profitable operation—and the inspiration for countless business books. Even entrepreneurs, it turns out, like a little craziness.

FUN *IS* PROFESSIONAL

Remember, working in a fish market is a pretty tough job. If employees in those conditions can still have fun and take care of business, then anyone can.

It's easy for any business to say, "We can't have fun. Fun isn't professional." But it just isn't true. Fun isn't an add-on to professionalism. Fun *is* professionalism.

As Richard Branson once said, "If you're *not* having fun, you might as well quit." The best way to have fun is keep trying new things. Keep surprising yourself. Keep learning. And above all, keep them talking.

THE YELLOW TUXOMETER

For each question, answer with one of the following: all the time (ten points), sometimes (five points), or never (one point).

1. How often do you laugh at work?

2. How often do you share ideas at work?

3. How often do you high-five your coworkers?

4. How often do you play games or have contests in the office?

THE YELLOW TUX BOOKSHELF

Welcome to Funderdome. If you've gotten this far, you know that fun is serious business here at Fans First. But don't just take my word for it. Here are some classic books on the art of fun.

- *Fun Is Good*, by Mike Veeck

- *Nuts*, by Kevin and Jackie Freiberg

- *When Fish Fly*, by John Yokoyama

CHAPTER *Eleven*

KEEP 'EM TALKING

When you're finished changing, you're finished.

—BENJAMIN FRANKLIN

Benjamin Franklin was everything—a founding father, an author, a printer, a politician, a freemason, a postmaster, a scientist, an inventor, a statesman, a diplomat, and more. He was and still is one of America's greatest entrepreneurs, famous for reinventing and redefining not only his numerous inventions and innovations, but also himself.

Welcome, my friend, to your final chapter, and my last task for your journey. It's time to make reinvention part of your DNA. Every moment of every day, I want you to be thinking about what you can do differently. Remember, as soon as it's easy, it's time to work harder.

Many businesses start off strong, but there's a reason why

96 percent of businesses fail within ten years. Eventually, they stop reinventing or creating anything new. That's the beginning of the end right there. When you stop caring, your customers stop caring too.

Even if you *do* still care, you've got to stay ahead just to keep up. No matter your business, your fans are constantly changing, and so must you. If you don't, you'll eventually be out of business. Like it or not, that's the harsh reality of it.

WHAT ARE YOU DOING DIFFERENT TODAY?

Too many business leaders take the rearview mirror approach to decision making. "Well," they'll say, "this worked last year, so let's do that same thing again."

Just because it worked once doesn't mean it will work again. In fact, it probably won't. Even if you loved what you did yesterday, even if your fans loved it too, it's time to do something new today.

I know, I know. Thinking up new things all the time can be stressful. That's why, like the fans-first, fun-first mentality we explored in the last chapter, you've got to make it part of your culture.

Ideas mean *a lot* to us. That's why we put so much emphasis on the Ideapalooza process that we talked about in
Chapter 4. We believe that by asking ourselves what we're
doing different today and every day, we create a solid
foundation to stand on tomorrow.

WHY DID THE CIRCUS SHUT DOWN?

Recently, after an incredibly long run of 146 years, the Ringling Brothers Circus shut down. But why? What happened?

The short answer is that it stopped being fun. Any circus
is built on the idea of fun and entertainment. You're supposed to show people things they can't see anywhere
else. But after 146 years, Ringling Brothers had long ago
stopped showing their fans anything new. They didn't
change with the times, and now they're gone.

FEAR OF IRRELEVANCE

Nothing weighs heavier on my mind than the idea of
becoming irrelevant. We've seen tremendous success
in a relatively short time at Fans First. Between our teams,
over a million fans have come through our gates to get a
taste of the show.

That's great, but here's the question: now that they've

already *seen* the show, what are we going to do next year to keep them coming back? How can we keep them talking with each new experience?

Eventually, fans will find our current brand of 24-7, non-stop entertainment boring. What then?

Perhaps we change the ballpark experience. How can I change the way people take in a game? How can I change the way they sit? What about the game itself? What can I do to create a new sense of excitement?

Maybe the answer isn't about the ballpark at all. Maybe our teams need to change how they take their show on the road. How can we bring the circus to other venues?

These considerations are doubly true for our frequent customers and season ticket holders. They see our show twenty-five times a year. It's a bit of balancing act to keep them happy. On the one hand, we can't keep trotting out the same promotions every night. On the other hand, we have to give them at least some sense of familiarity and consistency.

In a nine-inning baseball game, we have eighteen half-innings to fill. We have over a hundred promotions we rotate through, but we also have to constantly innovate with new ideas to keep things fresh. Ideally, even our season ticket holders see something different every game.

SMALL BETS: THE SECRET INGREDIENT TO REINVENTION

By now, you've probably noticed two things. One, I'm *really* invested in reinvention and doing things differently. Two, I don't always know the answers.

One thing I know is I won't get those answers by speculating about it here in this book. Instead, I'm using small bets as a proving ground for potential ways forward.

- 🖥 We've hired a full-time videographer and are constantly putting out new content to see how our fans respond.
- 🖥 We're hiring a full-time events director and director of operations to ramp up non-baseball events at the stadium.
- 🖥 We're looking at craft beer kickball leagues, concerts, morning beer fests, and movies in the park. Anything to bring fans in and give them a new kind of show.

As we learned with the Netflix story (see Chapter 7), sometimes you have to be open to changing your core competency. Right now, the games are our biggest draw, but that could change. We'll see if any of these small bets take us in a new direction.

THE NEW COKE TRAP

With all this talk about reinvention, you may be thinking, "Sure, Jesse, that all sounds good in theory. But what about New Coke?"

It's true, sometimes when you reinvent yourself, no one likes what you've become.

Everyone hated New Coke when it was first introduced. It was considered one of the biggest blunders in all of marketing history. However, when New Coke was pulled and Coca-Cola Classic was reintroduced, the brand became bigger than ever.

It was either a brilliant recovery or all part of a brilliant marketing plan.

The New Coke question boils down to this: What happens when your reinvention goes wrong? What happens when your fans don't like what you've become?

WHO ARE YOUR FANS?

At Fans First, we want to make our teams world-famous brands. Just like the Pike's Place Fish Market (see Chapter 10), we're intrinsically tied to our home cities. We have a responsibility to the fans in our community, and we take that responsibility very seriously.

However, to create a world-famous brand like P. T. Barnum, Warby Parker, or even the WWE, you have to treat everybody as a potential fan. You simply won't create the impact you want if you focus solely on your immediate community.

That means creating an identity that celebrates your home, but invites others in. Maybe that means taking your show on the road like Warby Parker, or maybe it means telling a story that people from around the world will want to be part of.

EXTENDING THE INVITATION

No one knew they wanted an iPhone before it came out. The smartphone reinvented the cell phone. For most people, it was an entirely new concept.

Apple knew this, and so they focused their marketing campaign on bringing people in, on making this new device seem so big and fun that everyone wanted to be part of it. They made customers feel like they had a choice.

We try to foster that same spirit with our teams. To keep people talking, you have to invite conversation. You have to prove time and again that you represent something fun, new, and different. And then, you invite them to come along.

YOUR FANS ARE ALWAYS CHANGING

If some of your fans don't want to come along, that's okay too. A lot of businesses focus on past customers. And while I'm certainly not going be the one to tell you to ignore them, there's more to the story.

You see, your customers are always changing. Unless you're Disney, you're not going to have the same fans for fifty or sixty years. Instead, you're going to have both younger and older fans who love what you do.

Try as you might, you won't be able to keep all your fans happy—or even keep all of them around. Some will get bored, some won't like the direction you're headed, and some won't think you're innovating fast enough.

It's a tough reality for any business to face, but the

truth is, your biggest fans today will not be your biggest fans tomorrow.

As Bill Veeck once said, your goal is to create the greatest enjoyment for the greatest amount of people. Right now, our teams entertain over a hundred thousand fans a year. We hope to keep reinventing so that in later years we can entertain one, two, maybe ten million people.

In the process, we'll lose some fans and gain some others. However, even if we don't change a thing, that's also going to be true. When you look at it that way, you have no reason not to take a risk and shake things up.

WATCH OUT FOR MAINTENANCE MODE

The longer you wait to reinvent, the more apparent your early shortcomings become. That's why you hear a lot of business leaders say that if you're not growing, you're dying. No one wants to find themselves in maintenance mode, as it can have a dramatic impact on your business's long-term success.

THE TOM'S SHOES LESSON

When Tom's Shoes hit the scene, they had a great vision and a great product, and it resonated deeply with their fans. They grew, and fast.

However, with great success comes the pressure of maintaining it. It's a lot of work, and it takes a lot of your time. Eventually, the people at Tom's realized they weren't taking chances anymore, which was too bad, because taking chances had been their calling card. Their culture had shifted. Instead of being excited about what they could *become*, they were only focused on what they were doing. Fortunately, they realized it, and the business eventually doubled down on their identity as risk takers and took their success to a whole new level.

DON'T FORGET THE LONG GAME

When you're maintaining, you're not playing the long game. You're not taking any risks.

However, the opposite can be true too. If you're *only* focused on the long term, you're not taking any small steps or making any small bets to create something new and fun.

The immediate long game in Gastonia is a new ballpark. I can't tell you how excited I am about this project. It's going to be the ballpark of the future, and it's going to once again change baseball in Gastonia.

However, that's about two years down the road. In the

meantime, what are we going to do for our fans to continue to create excitement? How do I prioritize making the next two years great for them, even though we're building toward something entirely different?

Change is never easy. It's a tricky balance we have to strike, but fortunately, I have a lot of smart people around me to help see everything through.

KEEP UP THOSE SMALL BETS

As Gastonia braces for its next big all-in moment two years from now, we're still making small bets to keep things loose and fun. This past season, during every live game, we broadcast a radio show that talks about everything going on at the ballpark—*except* the ball game.

These broadcasts are a little example of us sticking to our DNA and saying, "If it's normal, do the exact opposite." It's a small reinvention for now, but who knows what it could become down the road.

Just look at Gary Vaynerchuck. He didn't know he'd go from running the family wine business to heading up a huge media company. But one thing led to another. He took a small bet with his wine tasting videos, realized he had a flair for media production, and went all-in.

What you're doing now isn't necessarily what you're going to be doing later. My own career has seen dramatic role shifts—from college player to coach, GM, and owner. Five years from now, I might be reinvented as a traveling author and speaker. I might be wearing a new hat (or a new yellow top hat), but I'll still be doing what I do best—putting on a show and entertaining as many people as I can.

THE VEECK EFFECT

To the utter disappointment of business owners across the world, not every business will last. They may not fail—not completely—but they will fade. All good things must come to an end.

Bill Veeck made his career in baseball, but later he switched to new things, like horse racing. He continuously reinvented until the day he died. He never let his ideas die with him. Instead, he inspired others to go beyond a great launch. He inspired others not to stall.

BE THE SPOKESPERSON

How did he inspire others to keep talking? Well, he never stopped talking himself. By his own accounting, he gave about a speech a day—and sometimes as many as fifteen.

However, he never charged a dime for any of them.

Veeck had two reasons for never charging. First, he really liked to share and interact with others. This was apparent in every step of his career.

Second, he never shied away from self-promotion like a lot of entrepreneurs do. Honestly, a lot of entrepreneurs have trouble even talking about it, although it's hard to find a successful person who has never self-promoted.

Through his public appearances, Veeck was able to strike a good balance. He shared his passion and experience with others. By doing so, he gave back to the community. He also benefitted personally, however, because he was willing to put himself out there and talk about whatever he had going on at the time.

Veeck kept others talking about his businesses by always talking about them himself. He was a tremendous spokesperson, something he had in common with my other mentors, Walt Disney and P. T. Barnum. They all knew the best form of marketing was word of mouth, so they committed to sharing their vision with whoever would listen.

CONTROL THE CONVERSATION

The other benefit to Veeck's constant appearances is he controlled the conversation surrounding his businesses—and that conversation was all about passionately celebrating his teams and his fans.

After all, if you can't show you're excited about what you're doing, how can you get anyone else excited?

We follow this approach religiously at Fans First. Our social media posts are all about celebrating with the fans. You'll never hear us bring up a losing streak or a particularly tough loss. That's baseball. It's going to happen. We can't control it.

However, we *can* control the narrative around our team. And in that spirit, why highlight the negative parts? Who thinks it's fun to read about a losing streak? What about your winning streak of nine straight sellouts?

Keep your fans talking, but keep them talking about what *you* want them to be talking about. Don't highlight the negatives about your company unless you want others to as well.

GIVE 'EM ALL YOU'VE GOT

Bill Veeck once said about his ball games, "Every day is Mardi Gras, and every fan is king."

He meant every word.

To Veeck, every game was a huge event, and he did everything he could to build a media frenzy around it and get people talking. Just look at some of the promotions he was responsible for:

- He put on "Grandstand Manager's Night," where he let the fans dictate what would happen on the field.
- He once said, "I want people coming to the ballpark not knowing what to expect. The best things happen when you least expect it." To prove it, he never announced a fireworks show ahead of time.
- He gave away four thousand pickles to one fan and fifty thousand nuts and bolts to another. Then to top that, he gave a thousand hot dogs to one fan and a thousand buns to another.
- He would say, "The less it makes sense, the more it makes sense." To prove it, he staged a chariot race down at Suffolk Downs, his horse racing track—complete with real Hollywood props from the movie *Ben-Hur*.
- He and his son, Mike, staged "Disco Demolition Night,"

which was both a colossal success and a colossal failure. Fifty thousand fans descended on the ballpark, united in their hatred of disco. The ballpark turned into chaos, with fires, rioting, and the ever-present cloud of pot smoke. The White Sox had to forfeit because they couldn't keep their fans in line.

See how successful Veeck was at keeping people talking? I literally can't stop talking about him!

FANS FIRST—ALWAYS

I have to leave you with one more story, because it speaks not only to Veeck's pure, mad-scientist genius, but also to his deep, abiding love of his fans.

Once upon a time, a guy named Joe Early wrote a letter to the editor of his local newspaper. In it, he said something to the effect of, "How come the players get all the money and extravagant gifts? How come teams don't ever do anything for us regular fans?"

Well, Bill Veeck read that letter and said, "Challenge accepted." Not long after, he announced Joe Early night at the ballpark.

Veeck secured all sorts of donations from around the

community. Then, in front of a cheering crowd, Veeck presented Joe Early with a bevy of gifts. First, there was an outhouse. Then, an exploding carnival car that became a convertible, not to mention the other truck filled with gifts like a washing machine, a refrigerator, watches, and luggage.

People were so taken by the event that Early himself became something of a local celebrity, regularly giving interviews on TV and radio. Now, we may be Fans First Entertainment, but even we've never put a fan first quite like Veeck—at least, not yet.

CAN'T STOP, WON'T STOP

All the way up to his death in 1986, Veeck was always reinventing with new promotions and ideas. His autobiography, *Veeck as in Wreck*, was one of the first books I ever read, and it transformed the way I looked at sports and entertaining.

Most importantly, it challenged me to break myself out of the status quo.

In seventh grade, I would come home and have a Hot Pocket every day after school. In eighth grade, I swore them off for good, disgusted at the idea that I had done the same thing every day for over a year.

There's only so much you can have of the same thing, even if it's your favorite. Eventually, you must tell yourself, "You know what, it's okay to keep trying new things."

Not everything you try is going to stick. And not everyone is going to go along with you. But if you keep your eye on the long game and stay true to your mission, you're going to hit a lot more often than you miss.

Keeping your fans talking is about keeping things interesting. Everything in this book, from the first page to the last, has been about setting yourself apart from the competition. It's been about being unique and different.

In the end, it all boils down to this: a happy life and a happy business can be one and the same. All you must do is go all-in, get crazy with it, and believe in yourself.

THE YELLOW TUXOMETER

For each question, answer with one of the following:
all the time (ten points), sometimes (five points), or
never (one point).

1. How often is "It's always been done that way"
   said in your office?

2. When you first see the word "change," you get
   excited.

3. How often do you change your hairstyle or attire?

4. How often do you give speeches or presenta-
   tions about your business?

THE YELLOW TUX BOOKSHELF

In order to keep 'em talking, you've got to keep on reading—with these books that will keep you thinking.

- *There's a Customer Born Every Minute*, by Joe Vitalie

- *Marketing Outrageously*, by Jon Spoelstra

- *Buzz Marketing*, by Mark Hughes

- *Work Like You Are Showing Off*, by Joe Calloway

- *Unmistakable*, by Srinivas Rao

CONCLUSION

HOW DO YOU WANT TO
BE REMEMBERED?

People don't buy what you do. They buy why you do it.
—SIMON SINEK

Why do we do what we do at Fans First Entertainment?

Believe it or not, I didn't know the answer for years. I never gave it much thought.

One day during a conference I was attending, I watched Simon Sinek's famous TED Talk, "How Great Leaders Inspire Action."[28] I was so blown away that I immediately left the conference and spent the rest of the day watching the video on repeat.

---

28 Go ahead, give it a watch (Google keywords: "Simon Sinek TED Talk How Great Leaders Inspire Action").

It changed my life.

I showed the video to everyone after that—friends, family, employees, random strangers on the street, you name it.

Sinek's point was that people care more about *why* you do something than what you actually do. It made too much sense to ignore, so I began to ask myself about my own *why*. Gastonia had long ago embraced us as one of its own. We were creating fun. We were doing something unique. But what did it all amount to?

A MOMENT OF TRAGEDY—AND CLARITY

In 2011, tragedy struck Gastonia when a young man by the name of Nic O'Brien was killed overseas in Afghanistan. The news shook the small town to its core.

Within days, one of our interns approached me. "Jesse," she said, "I'm very close with the family. We need to do something."

"Yes, of course we do," I said. "Salute the Troops Night is in two weeks. Let's try to do something with that."

We reached out to the family immediately and asked if we could honor their son with a special tribute on the field.

They agreed, and Nic O'Brien's mother, father, sister, and girlfriend all came out to the ballpark to see their loved one be honored.

In the middle of the first inning, in front of a packed house of 3,700 people, we stopped the game and had the family come out onto the field. Two marines walked out with a special Nic O'Brien Grizzlies jersey and presented it to the parents. As we read our tribute to Nic, the entire crowd stood in silence.

You could hear a pin drop.

In ninety-degree weather, I had goose bumps.

When the family came off the field, Nic's mother gave me one of the biggest hugs I've ever received. I thanked her for her son's service and headed to my office.

Once inside, I lost it. For a young twenty-seven-year-old, the whole scene was too much to take—though in the best way possible.

During the tribute to Nic O'Brien, the entire stadium was one family. The feeling was both unmistakable and tremendously powerful.

In that moment, I began to realize why we do what we do—to bring people together. There is nothing more powerful than bringing a community together as family.

EVERY FAN IS FAMILY

Five years later, in our first season in Savannah, a mother of seven bought her family tickets to a Bananas game. However, whenever we tried to check in with her about the tickets, we never heard anything back.

Eventually, one of our staff members was able to get in touch with the husband. He shared that his wife had died tragically not long after buying the tickets, and the family was still in mourning.

After telling me everything that happened, the staff member asked, "What can we do?"

"Whatever you need to do," I said. "It's up to you."

Not missing a beat, he said, "What if we get a special jersey made of the mother? The number can represent the number of years she and her husband were together. We can present him with the jersey when they show up, and then we do everything we can to create an unbelievable experience for them."

It was a great plan.

When they came out to the game, the Bananas players all presented the kids with signed bats and balls along with the jersey, and then we gave them the show of their lives.

The father wrote to us a few days later. He said the tickets were the last gift his wife would ever give her kids, and he couldn't have imagined a better gift and experience.

These are always tough moments that we share with our staff. Tragedies like this make what we do seem so small, but also so big. Our fans have decided to trust us with these moments and welcome us into their lives, and it is an honor we do not take lightly.

HOW I WANT TO BE REMEMBERED

Ultimately your *why*, your reason for doing everything you do, is how you're going to be remembered.

Even after realizing the why of the business was to create family, I had trouble thinking about how I wanted to be remembered. It's a big question—and not a particularly comfortable one.

However, if I'm going to wrap up this book encouraging

you to think deeply about yourself, I'd better put my money where my mouth is.

TERMINAL DAYS

It took me several false starts to get it all written down. I'd sit down and scribble out anything that came to mind, but it didn't feel real. It didn't feel authentic to who I am.

Looking for inspiration, I turned to another thought leader I love, Ricardo Semler. On Mondays and Thursdays, Semler learns how to die. During what he calls his "terminal days," he envisions a doctor telling him he only has a short time to live. Then, he spends the rest of the day doing things he'd always wanted to do, but had never got around to.

I found this fascinating. While I don't feel the need to pretend I'm going to die twice a week, I love the fundamental question that Semler is asking: how would you live if you knew you were going to die?

When I asked this of myself, my first thought was not necessarily how I would live, but rather what I would regret. I know I'm not alone in this. A lot of people fear the regrets they will take with them to their deathbed.

Most people regret the things they've never done—the

opportunities they never took, the what-ifs, the worlds and experiences they were too afraid to explore. I get scared even writing about it here.

TAKE THE CHANCE

On the other hand, I rarely regret looking back on the chances *I did take*. Even if I failed, at least I learned something from it, and usually that failure led to some greater success down the road.

Semler's approach is powerful because it forces us to start with the end in mind. Like Semler, Gary Vaynerchuck says the key to success is to reverse engineer your life. Stop living day by day. Go to the end. Picture what your fulfilling life looks like, and write down the steps it will take to get there.

As baseball's greatest quote machine, Yogi Berra, once said, "If you don't know where you are going, you'll end up someplace else." Most people don't know where they're going. It's a terrifying feeling. However, as Geoff Blades says in *Do What You Want*, all you have to do to live the life of your dreams is to keep moving forward.

WHAT IF YOU WERE TO DIE TODAY?

If you died today, would you be content with the life you lived, or would you die with regret? What would your funeral look like? Who would be there? How *many* people would be there? How would you have impacted their lives?

With this framework in mind, I started over. This time, I wrote everything out in past tense, pretending I'd already passed from the earth. That gave it more meaning. If I was already gone, what would I want friends, family, coworkers, and strangers to say about me?

Eventually, as morbid as it sounds, I came up with the eulogy that I used to open this book:

> *Jesse Cole was the ultimate showman who entertained millions by bringing energy, enthusiasm, and enjoyment to everything he touched. A person who inspired millions to challenge the status quo, to be different, and to live the life of their dreams. A person who truly cared for others, was always there for anyone, who would give them everything he had. And the most loving husband and father to his wife and kids. He devoted his life to them and made them happy.*

My eulogy could change in a few years. It probably will. But for now, it keeps me accountable—both to myself, and to you.

START SOMETHING THAT MATTERS

It took a while for Fans First Entertainment to figure out and live up to our *why*. Other companies know right off the bat.

Toms Shoes founder Blake Mycoskie knew their *why* from the very beginning: to give back, to start something that matters. They achieved this with a simple business approach. For every pair of shoes a customer bought, Toms would donate a pair to a community in need. From this basic idea, their founder was able to grow a $300 million company that has helped countless lives.

Unfortunately, their *why* got lost along the way. Toms had become so successful that they focused all their energy on growth. One day, Mycoskie realized two things: (1) he wasn't enjoying himself at the company anymore, and (2) the company had lost sight of their mission.

With a renewed focus, Mycoskie returned to work and began investing in meaningful, purpose-based startups and companies—including ventures in coffee and drinking water. Some of Toms' top people quit in protest, but Mycoskie's vision was right. Rather than hinder Toms' growth, it accelerated it.

WHAT ABOUT YOU?

Blake Mycoskie didn't want to be remembered as the founder of a billion-dollar company. He wanted to be remembered as somebody who gave back. And by focusing on that, he was able to have a greater impact than even he imagined.

So, here it is. You've heard about Toms Shoes, Fans First Entertainment, and even me, the Yellow Tux Guy.

What about you? Why do *you* do what you do? How do *you* want to be remembered?

It's okay if you're not sure yet. I wasn't either at first.

In the meantime, don't waste your time sitting around and thinking about it. Get out there and start trying new things.

To paraphrase a brilliant philosopher named Will Ferrell, keep throwing darts at the dartboard. You'll eventually hit the bull's-eye.[29]

Just remember this, whatever you do, don't just do it for yourself. Think about the impact you have on others. Think about the impact you want to have on others.

---

29 Ferrell gave this gem of advice toward the end of a great 2017 commencement speech at USC (YouTube keywords: "Will Ferrell USC Commencement Speech 2017").

Focus on significance, not success.

Be remembered for *who you are*, not for what you've accomplished.

As Walt Disney said, "All of our dreams can come true, if we have the courage to pursue them."

Stop standing still. Start standing out.

THE YELLOW TUXOMETER

There's no point system for this last set of questions. Your answers are your own.

1. What does your extraordinary life look like?

2. What's holding you back from achieving it?

3. How will you be remembered?

Write down whatever you like here. Just make your answers count, and then make them a reality.

THE YELLOW TUX BOOKSHELF

I know, I know—parting is such sweet sorrow. Our time here may be up, but that doesn't mean I can't leave you with one last parting gift—or in this case, these five parting gifts.

- *How Will You Measure Your Life?*, by Clayton Christiansen

- *The Carpenter*, by Jon Gordon

- *Leave Your Legacy*, by Ben Newman

- *Everybody Matters*, by Bob Chapman

- *Magic of Thinking Big*, by David Schwartz

ARE YOU READY TO YELLOW TUX YOUR LIFE?

Now that you've read the book and answered the questions at the end of each chapter, it's time to see where you stand. Head over to www.findyouryellowtux.com to find out how you did.

Also, if you enjoyed this book and think a friend or colleague might enjoy it, shoot me a note about who you think might deserve a copy, and I'll send you a free bonus for helping to spread the word.

You can email me at jesse@findyouryellowtux.com or call me at the Savannah Bananas International Headquarters at 912-712-2482.

GRATITUDE

It was March 9, 2016. I was driving down Franklin Boulevard in Gastonia when I received the call. It was from a blocked number. For some reason, I answered. There to greet me was a familiar British accent.

"Hello," the voice said, "this is Simon Sinek."

"Shut up. Who is this?" I replied. Most of my friends know Simon is one of my idols. I didn't believe it was actually him for a second.

But the voice on the other end insisted. He *was* Simon Sinek. And I was in shock.

We enjoyed a short, but amazing, conversation. As it turned out, Simon had called simply to thank me for the letter I wrote him. He told me how much it inspired him, that letters like mine are the reason why he does what he does.

If you are unfamiliar with Simon, look him up. His presentation, "How Great Leaders Inspire Action," is the second most popular TED Talk in the world. His books, *Start with Why*, *Leaders Eat Last*, and *Together Is Better*, are revolutionary works on leadership.

Anyway, the point of this story is not to brag about my talk with Simon. It's to share the power of thank you—and most importantly, the Thank You Experiment.

It started on January 1, 2016, shortly after I chose the word "care" to be my word of the year. I knew I needed something to keep me focused on caring every day. So, I decided I would embark on what I called the Thank You Experiment, a project that would see me writing a handwritten thank you letter every day of the year.

It changed my life. I wrote to former teachers, coaches, long-lost friends, authors, restaurant servers, business leaders, and musicians—anyone who I truly appreciated and who made an impact on my life—no matter how small or how big that impact was.

I wasn't looking for anything in return. I just wanted to let these people know that I cared.

Since then, the Thank You Experiment has graduated from an experiment to an essential part of my life. I make thank you letters, calls, and emails a part of my daily ritual. So, it would seem that writing out the acknowledgments for this book would be easy, since it has become so engrained in my life. Unfortunately, that is far from the case.

Hundreds of people have impacted my life—too many to name here. With that being said, the following individuals have had the greatest influence on my life and on this book.

First, I'd like to thank my wife, Emily Cole. You've read about the challenges we've overcome so far in our business and in our marriage. The reality is that almost all of them were imposed by me. Not only has she taken everything in stride, but she has also embraced every form of adversity possible. She truly is the most caring person in the world. She has supported me through everything, and she sacrifices herself for others every single day. She is the reason I've been able to find *my* yellow tux and share this book with the world.

Next, I'd like to thank my family, starting with my dad. I often get asked about the best advice I've ever received.

My answer always begins and ends with my dad. He's always been ready with great tips like, "Swing hard in case you hit it," and "Work hard, and the money and everything else will take care of itself." But more than that, he has lived his life in a way that continues to inspire and guide me.

I never realized what inspired me until my dad found out he had two forms of cancer. For an entire year, he endured round after round of chemotherapy as he fought back against the cancer invading his body. Every day, I'd call to see how he was doing. Every day, he had the same response, "I'm doing great, Jess." He would always say it with such energy and sincerity that I knew he was going to be fine. He would always say it was just a matter of time before he was back and feeling better than ever. He was right. It was just a matter of time. He defeated cancer and went into remission. He's now the healthiest and happiest I've ever seen him.

This lesson in positivity truly hit home with me. Positivity can defeat anything. My dad's positivity and optimism inspires me daily to be a better person, to not complain, and to always see the positive in everything. That is the root of this book.

Next up in my family is my stepmom, Diane. Since I was a kid, she has taught me so many lessons and made me stronger as a person. While I may not have always realized it at the time, she would challenge me on my beliefs not to fight with me, but because she cared. Because of you, I've learned when to stand up and challenge myself to think differently.

I would also like to thank the McDonald family for showing me what a large, caring family looks like. You have created a family structure that I didn't even know existed, one built solely on caring for each other and always being there for each other. Thank you for welcoming in the crazy guy in the yellow tux.

Thank you as well to our entire team at Fans First Entertainment, who have given me a deeper purpose than they know. The Fans First team teaches me something new every day and inspires me to be a better leader. They constantly make me laugh and call me out when I deserve it. But more than anything, they make me proud. I love you guys, and this book is because of you.

Now to thank some of my best friends. I'm not good at making decisions on who to name here. Even at my wedding, I couldn't name just one best man, so I had eleven. I'll start with you guys.

Ben Ouellette and Mike Eromin, you guys are the most

creative people I've ever met. Many of the crazy ideas that I come up with are inspired by you.

Steve Johnson, as a college roommate, you made life fun. These days, your constant support on Facebook means more than you know.

Andrew Welsch, you always make calls just to check in and see what's going on in my world. This isn't something people do much anymore in a world of texting and Snapchatting. Thank you, Andrew, for always being there, man!

Andrew Walsh, in order to not confuse you with Andrew Welsch, let's go with T-Bone, your nickname that has lived on since high school. As my older stepbrother (two months older), I've always looked up to you. You always know how to make people laugh, and some of the attempts at humor in this book I know were inspired from you.

Jason Shoemaker, you are my best bearded friend and have offered me more advice over the years than anyone. Thank you for this.

Alex, David, and Ben McDonald, while I've shared how much your family means to me, you guys have welcomed me in as a brother and supported me, my business, and all my crazy ideas. You guys are the definition of what brothers should be.

Jeremy Railton, you are possibly the best combination of hilarious and brilliant that I know. As my roommate for almost seven years after college, your support has brought me here.

"Raj Chapter." Raj, I didn't forget about that phone call when you told me, "I'll be damned if you don't name a chapter after me in the book." So, Raj, here is your chapter.

Thank you to the team at Book In A Box. When I first heard Tucker Max talk about Book In A Box, I was inspired and knew he was building something special to help people be heard in the world. To my first publisher, Holly Foreman; my developer, Mark Chait; my marketing genius, Charlie Hoehn; and my final publisher, Julie Arends—you guys are truly rock stars.

My editor, Chas Hoppe, deserves a lot more said than I can even say here. I can't tell you how many hours I spent with him going over ridiculous stories and revisions for this book. He is hilarious, unbelievably talented, and truly gets it. But more than anything, he became a great friend during this journey. As I shared with him, after every call, I truly felt like a better person ready to take on the world.

Chas, thanks for being there through this process, for listening to all my ideas and nonsense, and for making this dream a reality.

To Bill Veeck and Mike Veeck—first impressions make a huge impact. As I've shared in this book, *Veeck as in Wreck* was one of the first books I read when I started my career. And Mike Veeck offered me amazing advice during one of his conferences, and it changed my life. Thank you both for seeing the fun in everything and providing fun to millions.

To Mike Michalowicz, what started from just a thank you letter has turned into a great friendship. I've been inspired by your success and ability to inspire thousands of people. You have become a mentor to me. My first "Find Your Yellow Tux" speech started at your event, and it grew into this book.

To Ken and Bette Silver, for giving a kid just out of college a chance. You guys have and continue to be amazing mentors and parent figures to both Emily and me. To this day, I still want to make you both proud.

It sounds so cliché to thank the fans. But to the millions of people who have come to our ballparks, proudly worn our logos, and been there through the wins, losses, rain, and outrageous shenanigans, thank you from the bottom of my heart. The best part of every game for me will always be standing at the gate thanking you for coming. Whether it's taking selfies, shaking your hand, or giving hugs, it's these moments that matter most. Creating amazing experiences for you that make a difference in your life is why I do what I do. So, thank you for allowing me to put on a show every day and have the time of my life.

Finally, I want to thank everyone who has believed in someone throughout their life and has shared that with them. Often, all we need is a little encouragement to take the next step. Just a push here and there.

I get inspiration every day—from the hundreds of books I've read, the podcasts I listen to every morning, and the countless videos and TED Talks I've seen.

Every day, someone inspires me to be better. While these people may never realize it, their belief in me and in people as a whole are changing the world.

With that said, it's up to us to constantly try new things, put ourselves out there, and believe in something greater than ourselves.

Thank you all for believing in me.

ABOUT THE AUTHOR

JESSE COLE is the founder of Fans First Entertainment and owner of two multimillion-dollar baseball teams, the Gastonia Grizzlies and the Savannah Bananas. He's been featured on MSNBC and as a keynote speaker all over the country, promoting his motto, "If it's normal, do the exact opposite." He's the host of the *Business Done Differently* podcast.

Printed in the USA
CPSIA information can be obtained
at www.ICGtesting.com
LVHW021826061223
765753LV00004B/363